The Happy Campers

Tess Carr and Kat Heyes

BLOOMSBURY

for Fred, Karn, Jenny and Lizzie

Contents

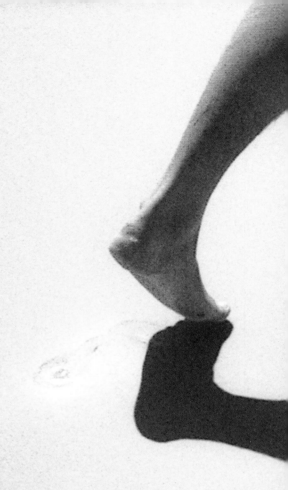

Introduction

happy camper: *noun* [c] HUMOROUS someone who is happy with the situation they are in; example: she's just found out she can't go away for the weekend and she's not a happy camper

Our inspiration

Long sunny days, sand dunes, running, jumping, long summer nights, gorgeous sunsets, sausage sarnies, big orange-frame tents, getting rained on but never remembering that bit, bonfire smoke, festivals, eating outside in the fresh air, fish and chips, bacon butties, melted marshmallows, shooting stars, the hot sun on your back while your front is roasted by the campfire, how good the wine tastes, loving your friends.

Our lives and loves

We've been camping since we were babies, year in year out, rain or shine, hot or cold. Though we hadn't yet met, we both grew up in the same beautiful part of Wales, close to Aberystwyth, in an area full of mountains, streams, lakes, beaches and perfect camping spots. A pretty amazing childhood for both of us, filled with happy memories, laughter and fun.

Then Kat met Fred, Tess's brother, and their romance began and so did our friendship – strengthened by our love of camping and eating. Many camping adventures followed and friendships flourished between us and many of our friends and family. Tess met and fell in love with her man, Karn, after he whisked her off camping on the Cornish coast. The happy camping circle just keeps on growing. We are now related by marriage: Fred proposed to Kat while travelling and camping in Australia and she very happily accepted.

We have camped on idyllic beaches, on mountains and moors, at festivals, in beautiful cottages and windmills, in forests and fells. We plan to keep on camping right into our golden years, surrounded by multitudes of grandchildren and maybe even great-grandchildren.

We wanted to write a book to share our experiences and what we have learnt and discovered along the way and pass on our love of happy camping.

The Happy Campers

Happy camping is a whole world of fun. It's not just about pitching a tent and bedding down for the night; there's so much more to it than that. For us it's a way of life: slowing down, living at nature's pace, enjoying friends and families, the excitement, the freedom, seeing the stars on a clear night, running to be the first in the sea, waking up in the morning to hear laughter . . . It's what really important in our hectic lives.

Are we nearly there yet?

Our book

The happy campers can be used by anyone, of any age and camping ability, from the novice campers just starting out right through to the more seasoned camper who might want to try some new things to make their camping trips even better.

Our main hope is that by sharing our love of camping, along with some of the ideas, flavours, sunsets, stories and discoveries that have made our experiences so good, we will inspire you to make your own journeys and create your own unforgettable memories.

Camping memories

Everyone has a childhood memory of camping, whether it's of making a bed-sheet tent in the back garden or of a family camping trip with long summer evenings spent in front of a roaring campfire and being allowed to stay up late. Every now and then we come across a member of the 'glass half-empty' gang who remember camping being a total washout; but often with a little reflection even wet experiences can evoke a fondness or at least a chuckle. A friend of ours says that camping trips were his happiest times as a child. Tucked up in his warm bed, top-to-tail with his sister, and his mum and dad so close, it was as if his family was all that mattered in the world – and that gave him a real sense of security.

For both of us, camping has always been part of our lives. First making camps in the front garden and then in the field behind the house but always coming home for tea. Then there were camps with mum, dad, siblings and dogs. Later came camping with mates, being totally unprepared but not really caring because we were all in it together. And then finally learning the art of romantic camping, when everything had to be just perfect in order to make an impression (whether it was always the right impression is another story).

For us, finding a reason for us to camp has never been hard. Birthdays, summer holidays, weddings, festivals, honeymoons, Christmas, that rare sunny day in autumn, a bank holiday – any day. The point is you don't need an excuse; camping is about being free to do whatever you want, whenever you want.

Why camping is so great

What can we say – camping is the best! (yes, we know we sound like camping nerds, but it's true). It has so many plus points: you get to create so many happy memories, usually filled with laughter and adventure, it's exciting and has unpredictability about it – anything can happen; it's spontaneous, an adventure which starts before you've even left, and you can choose where you're going or simply drive and end up in a new part of the world.

Camping is brilliant because you get to enjoy your friends and family in their purest form, when they are at their most relaxed and happy. Think back to your childhood: those days spent camping were amazing as they were the time you got your parents all to yourself.

Being in the great outdoors surrounded by the countryside helps you to relax and value the small things – things like children laughing, the smell of the campfire, sandy feet and sunkissed faces. It's about waking your senses and feeling alive again. It's good for the soul.

Camping holidays are also cheap and easy to organise, great for everyone big and small. You can just pack up and head off for the weekend if the weather looks good or stay for longer and feel unbelievably relaxed when you get home.

It can be a social experience if you want it to be. You can hang out with other like-minded people; you can be alone with whoever you are camping with. It can be romantic – discovering new loves, fire-gazing and love-hearts abounding – or it can be a gathering of your nearest and dearest, laughing and larking about.

Camping strips us back to basics and gives us a glimpse of what's really precious in our lives: just enjoying the simple pleasures of food, good company and fun.

Not just in a tent

Camping doesn't just mean having a tent as a home. To us, it can just as easily mean pottering through the countryside on a barge, driving off into the sunset in a camper-van or setting down in a big old house with all your family and friends. In fact it means being anywhere that you can stay overnight, that takes you out of your usual surroundings and necessitates you providing for yourself. Nothing is quite the same as sleeping under canvas but the alternatives can nonetheless make a great base from which to explore the countryside and try new things. And the advantages are obvious in winter: you can step straight into nature, get blown about a bit and refreshed by the crisp air knowing that later you will be holed-up inside, happily toasting your feet on a roaring log fire.

Happy ever after

There is never a right way of camping, just your own way. Remember: a tent isn't just to keep you dry but is also a place for relaxation, resting in comfort, reading and entertaining. We think it's time for a new approach to camping – so forget about the expensive camping gear and the 'right' equipment and start thinking of camping as a way to finding freedom, fun and happiness.

Go on, pack your tent and come with us . . .

before you go

Are you a planner? Or are you going to be spontaneous, leaving it all to chance and seeing where you end up? Maybe you have half a plan . . .

Why are you going camping?

Camping is a great way to get away from it all and it just so happens that it's good on the pocket and the environment too. You get to squeeze as many holidays and breaks as possible into your summer – you can pretty much just pack up and go every weekend if you like. You can see the world and celebrate the special times. Maybe you're going to a festival? Maybe you're organising someone's birthday or hen night? Don't forget that camping can be an option if you're going to a wedding. Just remember to take a few little luxuries to make it super special.

Where do you want to visit?

Have you got somewhere in mind – either a place that has been recommended or maybe a place that you have always wanted to go to? Do you feel like going somewhere new or do you want to revisit somewhere you have fond memories of?

Part of the beauty of camping is that you really get to discover the natural diversity of our extraordinary island. Great Britain is, quite simply, beautiful. We haven't seen the half of it but we have been lucky enough to discover more than a few places that we now hold close to our hearts. Here are just a few of those.

North Norfolk

We've spent many a relaxing holiday in Norfolk visiting some of our lovely friends. The beaches are fantastic, with huge expanses of sand perfect for kite flying and games of volleyball – and there's even a chance you'll spot some seals. There is also so much fresh food on your doorstep; book a fishing trip from Wells or pick your own samphire straight off the beach. If catching your own feels like too much effort and you're in Burnham Market, pop in to our favourite fishmonger's and say hello from us.

Scotland

Unlike in the rest of the UK there are some parts of Scotland where you are free to camp anywhere – just be sure to leave no trace of your visit and follow our wild-camping code (see page 29). There is such peace and tranquillity, because it's so easy to get off the beaten track and not see anyone else for days. The scenery is awe-inspiring and is best enjoyed out of your car, on foot, horse, bike or kayak. The crystal-clear lochs are ideal for all sorts of water sports. And then there's always the whisky . . .

The New Forest

Just down the road road from where we live now is a haven of wilderness and tranquillity. The dreamy New Forest, with its free-roaming ponies and ancient woodland full of tall oaks, horse chestnuts and spreading beech trees, is a lovely place to stay and find yourself cocooned by nature. You can't camp freely but there are lots of well-run private sites and some quieter wilder sites with no facilities that are run by the

Forestry commission. Nearby are the beaches of Dorset's towering jurassic coast, which are great for a bit of fossil hunting or lazing away summer afternoons.

Cornwall

One thing that Cornwall does is make an impression on you. There's something about the place that spreads a little love. Certainly it spread some our way: Tess fell in love with the man of her dreams there and Kat married the man of her dreams there – so watch out!

Cornwall has its own microclimate going on and as well as being perfect for camping the mild weather makes for a beautiful, rolling, country-garden landscape tinged with exotic palms and tree ferns. Spectacular cliff walks with stunning views run for miles alongside its stretches of golden sand and secret coves. The geographical variety of coast means that you're never far from the right beach for swimming, surfing, sailing, sand boarding, dog walking, kite surfing, snorkelling or just lying about doing not very much at all. Learning to surf in Cornwall is really good fun and right on the beach-fronts you'll find numerous places hiring out wetsuits and swell boards (learner boards that don't hurt when the wave gets you) and many surf schools to help you on your way. Don't feel intimidated – just get out there and have a go. We guarantee that afterwards you'll feel like you really deserve that third pasty of the day.

The Scilly Isles

If you're in Cornwall you must try to fly or ferry across to this little group of islands for some gorgeous tropical white beaches. The Scilly Isles are amazing for camping but you can't take too much stuff because no cars are allowed. This makes them ideal for a spontaneous trip with your lover as you don't need much more than each other.

Devon

And don't forget to visit Devon for the clotted-cream teas, native wild ponies, mysterious granite tors, ancient myths, ghost stories, and the lovely local accents.

The Lake District

The Lake District is fantastic because it comprises lots of different landscapes within one area. You can experience the serenity of the valleys and lakes while surrounded by the high crags of the fells (the mountains of the Lake District) or follow a ghyll (a mountain stream), up to a tarn (a small lake, generally higher up) for a picnic and an afternoon swim. Seek out the campsites situated near to the lakes, which are incredibly picturesque. You'll probably find yourself in the company of some locals – Herdwick sheep, which are indigenous to the area.

Wales

The playground of both our childhoods, Wales is known for its wet weather but – trust us – it can get some amazing periods of dry, sunny weather and, thanks to all those April showers, the stunning landscape is possibly the most lush green in the whole of Great Britain. You can do almost any sporting activity you could wish for, from hill walking and kayaking to gorge walking and coast steering, but simply enjoying some of the free stuff that Wales has to offer is the main attraction for us. Its mix of rolling green hills and spectacular mountain ranges are dotted with waterfalls, caves, potholes and deep, wooded gorges ripe for exploring. Some of our most treasured memories are of being true water babies, enjoying the natural rock pools and slides in the crystal-clear water of Wales's abundant rivers, and of playing away on long summer days on one of her many beautiful beaches.

Ireland

Ireland is quite similar, in many ways, to Wales, with its lush green expanses, idyllic scenery and magnificent seascapes. The climate is similar too, but what Ireland lacks in constant sunshine it more than makes up for in character. The north coast, framed by the Atlantic Ocean, is steeped in history and choc-a-block full of wildlife. Opportunities for horse riding, hiking and cycling are plentiful and it's becoming an increasingly popular location for surfers. The Mourne Mountains, in an area of outstanding natural beauty, provide a lovely backdrop to any camping trip and there are also some quaint islands off the coast which make a wonderful escape. If you're a hunter-gatherer type, Ireland has some of the best fishing spots on offer. When you have had enough of the great outdoors you can take advantage of the friendly welcome in your nearest watering hole – and of course there's no shortage of these either. There you can indulge in what Ireland is best known for, comforted by the heat of real peat fires when the weather gets you down and you've got the camping blues. You can be sure that the endless folklore and Guinness will prove a great pick-me-up.

When are you going to camp?

Another thing to consider is when you are going to go camping. If you're brave enough you can of course camp all year round, but you can never really depend on the great British weather so it helps to be prepared.

Spring is great. With buds on trees, flowers popping up and spring lambs dotting the fields, it is a real joy to celebrate the end of the dark days of winter by getting out of the house and going camping when new life is appearing everywhere and the campsites aren't that busy. A woodland camp is great in spring because the trees offer shelter from any wind but the sun can still get through where the leaves haven't yet appeared.

Summer is obviously the best time of year for camping. Hot, hazy summer days, lying back listening to the hum of busy insects and making cloud shapes. A lot of campsites do get very busy during the school holidays, especially at weekends and over the August bank holiday, so book ahead if you want to go somewhere specific. Every type of camp is great in summer.

In autumn you can enjoy cool, clear evenings, amazing sunsets, no insects, fewer people and the glorious seasonal colours. Beach camps are great in early autumn because the kids are back at school and the summer weather seems to last longer every year.

It's possible to enjoy camping in winter but you do have to be prepared. It's all about setting up home somewhere new and getting into the great outdoors. If the thought of a tent is just too much, why not hire a tipi or yurt and cosy up next to the fire? Or you could hire a cottage – much cheaper than usual at this time of the year and a great break away. You can still have a fire outside on which to toast your marshmallows and eat your mince pies around.

Finding a campsite

So you've thought about where you're going and how you're going to get there. Now, unless you're wild camping, you need to find a campsite. The romantics among us tend to have pretty high expectations – perhaps hoping to discover a picturesque, lakeside campsite where they'll drop off to sleep to the sound of water lapping outside, having spent the evening beside a roaring campfire with just their friends and the countryside for company. Unfortunately the reality can be quite different so it's wise to do a bit of research in advance to avoid disappointment.

The good old British campsite

Campsites in the UK generally fall into one of two categories. There are the larger holiday parks which usually accept caravans and tents and have many facilities, or there are the smaller, cheaper and much more basic sites.

Some of the larger campsites can feel a bit overcrowded. Many have everything from swimming pools and crèches to laundry services, bars and shops, which can be great if that's the sort of camping experience you're looking for. But, for us, the beauty of camping is in enjoying nature and all it has to offer. For a wilder camping experience it is definitely worthwhile seeking out the more basic campsites, those that offer a real sense of tranquillity. You'll often find that such campsites are fairly easy-going in terms of rules and regulations; so, while facilities might be limited to a basic toilet block and shower, it is quite possible that you'll be allowed to build a campfire and that the size of your pitch won't be restricted. This sort of campsite tends to be located in the country's wilder areas, such as West Wales and Scotland, but if you look carefully you'll find them dotted all over Britain. We have come across some great spots in West Sussex, North Norfolk, Cornwall and the New Forest and hopefully more will appear as the camping revolution gets under way. We once stayed on a lovely Welsh campsite comprising of just a shed in the middle of the field, where the owner made fried breakfasts and did Elvis impersonations every morning. Priceless!

Follow our top tips for choosing a campsite:
*   Ask locals for any recommendations, as a lot of the best campsites don't advertise.
*   Speak to other campers for those secret, word-of-mouth gems.
*   Check camping websites for campsite reviews.
*   Explore. Drive around, looking for hidden campsites away from busy roads – sometimes the best places are those you simply happen upon.
*   Book well in advance, especially in summer during the school-holiday period.
*   Check what facilities are on offer and how big the pitches are. Try to get a feel of the way the site is run. You can do this over the phone or on their website if they have one. Some campsites have a noise policy – worth checking if you intend to make noise or if you don't want to listen to someone else's. Also ensure that any other specific needs can be accommodated; for example, is there disabled access, is the site dog-friendly, kid-friendly, campfire-friendly, etc.?
*   Check out the listings at the back of this book for helpful places to begin your search.

Wild camping

One of our favourite ways to camp is to go wild. This means having your own little bit of the earth all to yourself and you can really get away from it all and enjoy the peace.

Unfortunately in England and Wales it is illegal to camp anywhere you like, unless you first ask the landowner's permission. However, in some upland and remote areas wild camping is tolerated. The laws are different in Scotland, where in some areas wild camping is openly allowed. It is best to do your research before you go, and to make sure you speak to the landowner before setting up camp – if you don't know who the land belongs to, ask local residents. You don't want to be woken early in the morning by an angry farmer.

Lots of people own small areas of pasture or woodland purely for the pleasure and many farmers and landowners can be very generous and accommodating with their land. Some rent out fields to campers but don't advertise, so you might just strike it lucky. We have had some fantastic free camps by politely asking the landowner and they have been truly amazing, even providing us with wood for our fire.

And, of course, you can also enjoy a wild camp if you are lucky enough to know someone who owns some land and is happy for you to use it.

Wherever you end up wild camping, though, you should bear in mind some important rules. So do remember to camp as unobtrusively as possible, respect the countryside and follow the wild-camping code.

The wild-camping code
- Respect the fact that people live off the land.
- Light a fire only if you have permission.
- Be considerate to others – including our furry and feathered friends.
- Remember your toilet etiquette (see page 79).
- Enjoy the freedom but leave no trace of your visit.

Practicalities

When we go camping we find that the more we take the comfier we feel so we end up taking everything, including the kitchen sink – well, the washing-up bowl. In fact, the more we camp the more stuff we seem to take with us. It could be something to do with getting older and needing more home comforts (though that wouldn't explain why Tess's mum, Jenny, still just rambles off with her fella, a two-man tent and a backpack). Whatever, it doesn't go down too well with our boys, as they are usually roped in to pack most of it, but we feel it's important to add that comfortable touch to our holidays and they are always thankful when we get there. Lying by the campfire on that comfy sheepskin you've remembered to bring and then climbing into the cosiest camping bed ever is one of the little luxuries we really look forward to.

We love making camp a real home from home, with little touches like flowers in the camp kitchen and tea-lights in the trees. But first things first, though. If you're a virgin camper and are without even basic equipment you need to find the fundamentals, like a tent and a stove, before you worry about tea-lights. Perhaps you have a friend who'd be willing to lend you some stuff, on the condition that you'll make good on any damage; even better, go camping with that friend and share – you'll probably have more fun and pick up some tips along the way. Don't worry too much about having specialist kit, either: old pots and pans will do and even odd china is so much nicer than plastic. Older tents are great fun and just as reliable for summer camping as brand-new versions. Look out for stuff in charity shop or car-boot sales, as many a camp stove and griddle pan have been found that way.

Tents

When camping probably the most important piece of equipment is your trusty tent, your home from home under the stars. We have had and stayed in many different types of tents over the years. When we were kids we both had those lovely old frame tents in delicious 1970s green and orange. We've since had two-man tents, frame tents, tents with pods, tunnel tents and dome tents. Almost every year, though, tent envy strikes when someone turns up with a new tent that's even bigger and better than its predecessors. Tess's most recent purchase was a lovely bell tent, which is a very striking number in canvas. It's like a tardis and is a beautiful space to wake up in. Kat is experiencing an extreme case of tent envy.

What type of tent do you want?

Frame tents are the typical 1970s family tent. Both of our frame tents came with bay windows and flowery curtains. They give the best headroom and living space and you can make separate compartments for bedrooms. They are very robust but also heavy so you won't be carrying it far from the car. Kat still sometimes uses the frame tent her family took on holiday all those years ago, as it can accommodate huge beds and is a perfect space in which to entertain guests on wet-weather poker days. When it's not practical to take the big house Fred and Kat take the lightweight three-man dome tent they picked up when camping along the east coast of Australia.

Dome tents are currently the most popular tents. They come in a multitude of sizes and are very simple to put up, using lightweight poles that thread through a sleeve in the tent fabric. They generally have a good amount of space inside and pack up small so you can hide them away in a cupboard until your next camping trip.

You can get all sorts of weird and wonderful dome tents with an amazing amount of sleeping pods attached. Our friend Grace has a three-pod tent with a living area in the middle all to herself, so she can have a dedicated cosy bedroom, store loads of luxuries and even entertain in what she likes to refer to as her west wing.

Geodesic tents are similar to dome tents but with strengthening along the sides. You might consider buying one if you know you're going to be doing a lot of winter camping or camping in very windy weather.

Ridge or frame tents are the traditional, classic, triangular-shaped tents (if you were asked to draw a tent this is what you would probably come up with). They provide really good protection from all types of bad weather, but there's not much headroom inside.

Tunnel tents are very lightweight tents that are hung from arched poles and form their shape when pegged out. These are very light and pack up small so are good if you need to walk, cycle or horse ride to your campsite. Before she got the bell tent Tess had a four-man tunnel tent. It was brilliant because it was very tall, which meant it had a huge porch that made a perfect kitchen space and there was height enough for her tall boyfriend Karn to stand up in.

Canvas fabric tents are a joy to spend time in. You can get lots of different canvas tents, from various-shaped scout tents to specialised one-pole tipi-style tents, and they all have the same spacious, tranquil feeling. Because they are made of just one layer of canvas the temperature inside can be a little cooler than in a nylon tent, but this can be an advantage on a hot summer's day. Some can be fitted with a stove or open fire. Bear in mind, however, if you're tempted to rush out and buy one, that they are much heavier and bulkier than their nylon counterparts. Canvas bell tents are really roomy – there can be enough space inside for a double bed, a kitchen area and even a hanging area for the all-important party frocks. They make a great alternative to tipis, very similar in atmosphere, but much easier to transport and erect.

There is an incredible range of tents and you'll find that some tents are very cheap, some are very expensive, some are easy to put up and some – unless you have a degree in tent construction – are almost impossible.

Deciding which tent to go for can be very confusing, so before you buy you need to ask yourself some questions:

How much money do you want to spend?
Set yourself a budget and weigh up all the pros and cons of each tent you like then work out which of them is the best value for money.

How often will you use it?
If you're a sporadic camper and your tent won't get much use, you could perhaps go for a cheaper option; if you're a regular camper it might be worth investing in something more expensive.

How many adults/kids/dogs will be sleeping in it?
Who is going to sleep where? Take tent-capacity ratings with a pinch of salt: for comfortable camping we'd always recommend getting a tent at least one person bigger than the stated tent size. You will also need to consider whether you'll be camping with friends in the future and might need room enough for entertaining or do you just want the space for yourself and your belongings.

If you have a family, do you want to sleep all together or give your kids their own tent?
They will love the independence of their first house and you can have some privacy. Remember, when camping, romance is never dead.

Is headroom important to you?
Tall people are more comfortable in tall tents. Whatever your size it's nice to have a porch tall enough to stand up in so you can hang out outside even when the weather's not up to scratch.

Will you be camping all year round?

If you're a summer camper you might not need a particularly sturdy tent, but if you intend to camp in the autumn or even brave it in winter it's a good idea to get something strong and more weatherproof.

Do you want to sleep under nylon or canvas?

Nylon tents are lighter, easier to carry, easier to put up and generally more wind- and waterproof than canvas tents but they can be sweaty and not as durable. Canvas tents are especially brilliant in the summer, being cooler and more spacious, but they are also cumbersome, so harder to carry, and take slightly longer to erect.

Do you have a car?

If you'll be driving with your gear you can get a bigger, heavier tent but if you're going to be on foot weight and size are very important. Tent poles come in a variety of materials which can affect the overall weight of the tent.

What colour do you like?

This may seem like a very girlie thing to say but it's always nice to wake up in an environment that makes you feel relaxed. Darker colours offer more shade from the morning sun but also make for a hotter tent later in the day.

You need to consider how fire retardant your tent is, whether there are any handy storage pockets or windows, how waterproof it is and whether it has any built-in sun protection. You should find out if the poles are colour coded to make it easier to put up (if not, and you think it would help, you could perhaps colour code them yourself when you first erect the tent at home).

A good idea is to go to a camping show or a showroom where you can see tents already erected. You can really get a feel for each tent, because you can go inside and get excited about all the fun to come. (The downside of doing this is that you'll inevitably fall in love with the biggest and/or best model and your budget will go straight out the window.) You should thoroughly test the zips to see if they are good quality, and check whether they are non-rusting. Make sure, too, that the fly sheet has strong seams. If you're a proper tent nerd, read through the instruction leaflet to make sure it's easy to understand. Most importantly, talk to the shop or show assistant about what they would recommend and why. Ask them for tips for putting the tents up, and for any campsite recommendations if you're planning to camp locally.

There is now a vast choice of tents on the internet and the increasing popularity of camping means that prices are becoming more reasonable – which is great news for all of us happy campers.

When you buy your tent you might want to invest in a few accessories to help you out. A mallet can be very handy to save hurting your hands if the campground is a bit on the firm side (though you can always use a rock or log). It's also useful to buy extra tent pegs because there are never enough and someone always forgets theirs.

If you have a new tent – and especially if it's your first time camping – try setting it up in the garden or park to see how it all works. This is a great excuse for an impromptu camp out! And if the tent proves unexpectedly big or small, or something is missing or its impossible to put up, then you'll have time to take it back and change it – just check the store policy before you buy.

Laugh more, love more, camp more . . .

Stoves

There is a massive range of stoves available in all different shapes and sizes, from the very cheap through to the very expensive. To discuss them all would take forever and you would probably fall asleep out of boredom reading it, so here is what you should consider when buying a stove.

What to consider when buying a stove
*   How many people you will have to feed?
*   Do you like creating gourmet meals?
*   How many burners do you want?
*   How long does it take to boil water?
*   How much do you want to spend?
*   How environmentally friendly is it?
*   Is the fuel a renewable resource?

Size and weight of the stove

Stoves can vary in weight from few hundred grams to a couple of kilos so check what the weight stated includes – does it include the fuel cartridge, canister or bottle?

Multi-burners

In our view, if you're going in a car, a multi-burner is definitely the best option because you can cook great meals on them and make tea at the same time. Look for ones with the following extras: grill; push-button ignition; adjustable flame; wind-shield and carry case.

Single burners

Small single-burner stoves are good if there is just one or two of you camping. If you're going backpacking there are specialist lightweight single burners available.

Fuel

Check how available the fuel is, and how easy it is to get refills and how much refills cost. If your stove uses cartridges you might not be able to refill them; consider how this impacts on the environments (for example, can you recycle the canisters?). You also need to know how hot the fuel will burn – this determines the performance of the stove. Finally, if you are going to camp abroad, you must check that your stove's fuel will be available at your destination.

Where are we going to stay today?

Tent – big or small
Tipi
Winnebago
Yurt
Camper-van
Motor home
In the boot of our car
Barge
Windmill
Treehouse
Roundhouse
Lighthouse
Stately home
Castle
Gypsy caravan
Beach hut
Under the stars

If not a tent, where?

Whether you're hiring a camper-van or a castle it's important to find out what will be provide for your stay. You may need to take extra bedding, towels, crockery, kitchen equipment and little luxuries like a coffee percolator or extra comfy stuff. In terms of finding cool places to stay, the internet is an invaluable mine of information. Most websites include photos and many have star ratings, so depending on your budget it's very easy to find what's right for you. Local tourist boards can also provide lots of information on accommodation, and most will send you free brochures packed full of ideas. Check the back of this book for more help with this.

Tipis and yurts

If you want to have the camping experience but fancy something extra special, why not hire a tipi (a traditional American Indian-style tent usually with a fire or stove in the middle) or a yurt (a traditional Mongolian-style tent, again with a stove)? There are a few independent companies that hire out both and they are now popular enough for a number of campsites and festivals to have them already set up for use. Tipis are beautiful spaces to be in – brilliant for families or groups of friends, but also very romantic if you fancy a getaway. Yurts are just as special. We hired one for a hen weekend and had it set up in a friend's garden. We cooked a massive feast and stayed up till the early hours playing Mr & Mrs and other 'embarrass the bride-to-be' games, then all fell asleep packed together like sardines, warmed by the wood-burning stove.

Before hiring a tipi or yurt, you should find out if it has a stove or a fire, if there's wood or other fuel provided and, importantly, if you'll be given instructions on how to erect it and light the fire if there is one.

Somewhere a bit different

There are so many different and unusual types of places to stay – log cabins, gypsy caravans, barns, bunk houses, windmills, lighthouses . . . Out of season you can even hire whole youth hostels. Often friends or work colleagues can divulge the whereabouts of some gem of a place. Keep your eyes peeled when on day trips to areas you think you might one day like to visit for longer. One winter drive in North Norfolk we stumbled across a windmill for hire that ended up being a fantastic Christmas camp.

Barges and narrowboats

How about hiring a barge or a narrowboat? They are brilliant fun and a unique way to pootle along and view the British countryside from a different perspective. You can take the tent if you want to pitch up when you moor, and if the weather's hot you can sleep on the roof of the boat.

Check in advance whether lifejackets are provided for poor swimmers and children, whether you'll have instruction on how to operate the boat and locks and whether you get a map. You should find out where the moorings are on your chosen route and plan ahead so you can get supplies along the way. Also enquire about cooking facilities and, if relevant, ask if you can take bikes on board. Crucially, try to find out where the best pubs are en route.

You got wheels

And, of course, there are caravans, motor homes and camper-vans. We love camper-vans. You might be lucky enough to own one but you can also hire them. They give you so much freedom, and yet you hardly have to pack. They are great if you don't want to plan your destination – just park up and sleep anywhere.

Motor homes are a bit more restrictive as they are generally bigger so a little harder to manoeuvre and they also need more power (and fuel). On the plus side, you get a lot more room and often more comfort as well.

Caravans have a dowdy reputation but we love them and are both dying to get our hands on an Airstream one day. You can hire these, too, and they are great for touring and longer expeditions.

Both motorbikes and bikes are great transport for camping trips as they give you so much freedom. Motorbikes offer you the excitement of real spontaneity and bikes offer you the chance to get right off the beaten track. Just remember to pack light.

If you've never towed a caravan or driven a motor home you'll need to have some instructions on how they operate. You'll obviously have to check whether you need to adapt your car in order to tow a caravan and what the rules of the road are.

The Happy Campers' essential checklists

These checklists (yes, we love lists) have been devised and revised throughout our camping adventures. Hopefully they will help you to remember those little things we have forgotten in the past. They are by no means set in stone and we use them at our discretion, so please feel free to do the same.

Main essentials

This is a list of our basic essentials; we don't necessarily take everything and what we do take is dictated by where we're going and who we're going with.

Tent and tent pegs

Bedding and mattress

Torch with extra batteries

Head torch

Mallet and spare tent pegs

Toilet roll and unscented soap/organic wet wipes

Road map and map of the local area

Mobile phone/extra battery or car adapter

Wash bag, including toothbrush and toothpaste

and make-up for the girls (or boys)

Money, credit card, etc.

Swiss army knife

Lighter or matches

String, scissors, wire and pliers (for making things)

Tarpaulin (see page 56 for uses)

Camp lamp

Hacky sack (see page 195)

Water container filled with water

Rope and bungee cords

Towel

Sun cream, sun block and aloe vera

Insect repellent

Earplugs if you're a light sleeper

Condoms if you're not

Small medical kit, including antiseptic cream,

plasters and arnica cream (for bruises)

Swimming cossies, flip-flops and sunglasses

Warm clothes

Waterproofs and wellies

Comfy walking shoes

Camera and film

Bin bags

Candles

Something to sit on

Trowel or spade

Guitar

Common sense

The Happy Campers book

Kids

Dogs

Friends

Main kitchen essentials

This list is what we consider to be some basic kitchen items you might need to take, to help fill your camp with delicious food. Of course, kitchen equipment tends to be recipe-dependent so if need be you could probably muddle through without some of the following:

Cooking stove (you could take a disposable or portable barbecue too)

Barbecue grill tray, if campfires are allowed – you can take from your oven at home

At least two saucepans (one big one and one non-stick)

Frying pan

Washing-up bowl and washing-up liquid (biodegradable)

Coolbox or bucket filled with cold water (see page 56 for other uses)

Wooden spoons

Fish slice

S-hooks (meat hooks) for hanging things on

Big mixing bowls and/or salad bowls

One good big chopping knife

One good sharp fruit knife

Bread board

Coffee-maker

Flask

Lots of tea towels and hand towels

Scrubber and dishcloth

Big bowls to eat out of

Tin foil

Crockery – food tastes better off china

Glasses and mugs

Cutlery

Tongs

Masher (not just for potatoes – good for combining things)

Whisk

Can opener

Bottle opener

Red wine

Set of tupperware boxes for leftovers and picnics, etc.

A friend to do the washing up

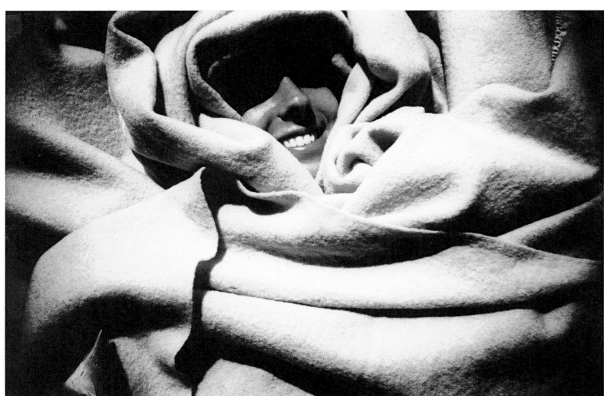

Essential extras

This is a list of those essentials that have given our trips that little something extra. It's not as though you won't survive without them, but we feel they are indispensable for a truly happy camping experience:

Loads of snuggly stuff – pillows, sheepskins, cushions, quilts – to make up your dream beds

Blankets for round the campfire

Nighties and pyjamas

Table and camp chairs

Picnic blankets and baskets

Cards and poker chips

Paper and pens

Frisbee, football, kites, cricket and rounders bats, swingball

Board games, other games and ingredients to make games (see Play chapter, page 170)

Gazebos and spare tents (you might need a dressing room)

Washing line and pegs

Dustpan and brush for sweeping your tent

Toys

Dressing-up stuff – wigs, tutus, indian headdresses, hats and frocks

Skipping ropes, batons and boules

Bubble machine

Water pistols (or recycled washing-up bottles)

Lilos

Lip balm

Books

Bikes

Wetsuit, snorkel and flippers

Camp decorations

Candlesticks, candles and tea-lights

Funny friends

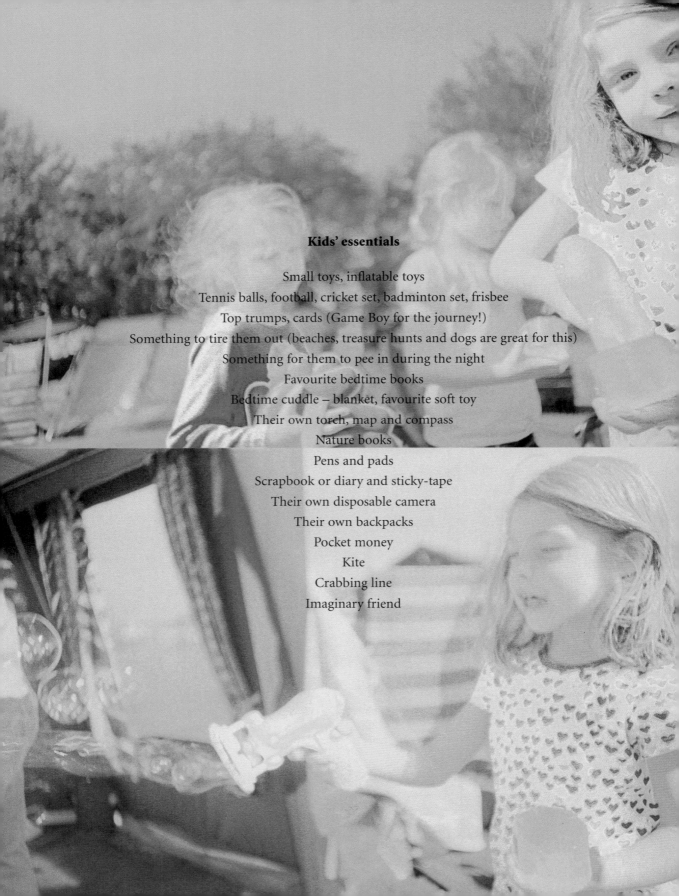

Kids' essentials

Small toys, inflatable toys
Tennis balls, football, cricket set, badminton set, frisbee
Top trumps, cards (Game Boy for the journey!)
Something to tire them out (beaches, treasure hunts and dogs are great for this)
Something for them to pee in during the night
Favourite bedtime books
Bedtime cuddle – blanket, favourite soft toy
Their own torch, map and compass
Nature books
Pens and pads
Scrapbook or diary and sticky-tape
Their own disposable camera
Their own backpacks
Pocket money
Kite
Crabbing line
Imaginary friend

Camping with kids

Camping with kids is so rewarding. They absolutely love it, tearing around, roaming free, entertaining themselves for hours in the biggest playground ever. They also get lots of attention, learn new stuff, make new friends and as a bonus, they're shattered at the end of the day from all that country air so you get some peace and quiet to enjoy the stars. If you're camping with kids for the first time, make your adventure a short one and don't go too far from home. Long trips can be disorientating and it takes most children a while to get used to lengthy car journeys – and you don't want to start your holiday with an unhappy baby.

Here are our top tips to keep your mini campers happy:
- Be organised and plan your trip.
- Properly research your choice of campsite, or visit one you've been to before, so you know what facilities are on offer.
- If you're taking teenagers allow them to bring a friend – much more fun for everyone.
- Don't go when the weather forecast is too hot or too cold.
- Packing more than you need is better than running out of anything.
- But don't worry if you forget something – you should be able to buy it locally.
- Plan to arrive well before dark, as setting up with children around takes twice as long. They will need time to explore and get used to their new surroundings.
- Take the kids' own bedding from home so they settle more easily at night.
- Plan some games and things to make but don't feel like you have to entertain them 24/7 – they will need some time for general larking about and exploring.
- Research the area for things to do on wet-weather days (see page 203).
- Give each child their own torch, to help them feel safe in the dark and to make shadow puppets on the tent walls with.
- Make sure that each child has their own bucket, spade, etc., in order to keep argument to a minimum.
- When you're going on a walk or doing something they consider 'boring', give each child a disposable camera to play with. Have the photos developed while you're away – it's a real treat for them, much more exciting than looking at mum or dad's digital-camera screen.
- Get them to collect feathers, flowers, leaves and other bits and bobs from nature to add to their photos and make a holiday scrapbook.
- To avoid putting little ones off camping for good, don't tell ghost stories before they go to bed – and remember that tent walls are not soundproof so don't tell them after they've gone to bed either.
- If they become scared of night-time noises reassure them that the countryside is naturally full of sounds; try not to investigate these sounds as this may give the impression that you're worried about them too.
- And, finally, don't forget: it's your holiday too, so get the kids involved. Washing up can be fun – honest!

Festival camping

Camping at festivals is brilliant fun. Buying your ticket, waiting for the days to pass, frantic emails and phone calls about who is bringing what, trying to get extra tickets at the last minute for those who want to come now because they're feeling left out.

At most festivals there's a great sense of camaraderie, and friendly mucking in together, especially if the weather gets dodgy. Festivals are also perfect opportunities to meet new people; if you spot someone you fancy you can always use the time-honoured camping chat-up line of asking to borrow their mallet.

For a smooth(ish) festival experience:
- Use our essentials list as a guide of what to bring (see page 46).
- Share the load: work out who is bringing what, so you don't end up with two of everything.
- Arrive early so you can get the best camp spot.
- Don't camp too close to the main action, so you can have your own bit of calm, but don't camp too far out or you'll have miles to trek across site.
- Avoid camping at the bottom of a slope or near the loos if you want to avoid getting wet or smelly or both.
- Rendezvous with your friends so that you can all camp next to each other. If someone will be arriving late, take their tent and put it up for them.
- Stick together – it's more fun. But don't forget to charge your mobile in case you do lose all your mates. Agree on a lost-persons meeting point in the event that there's no signal.
- Find a friend who has a vehicle pass and get them to take all your stuff on to the site. If that's not possible, take a wheelbarrow or trolley to make lugging it all easier.
- Girls, go with boys who have strong arms – they are very good at carrying and quite nice to look at. Boys, go with girls who have strong arms – they are also quite nice to look at.
- Create a central area and put the tents around it in a close circle. However, don't be greedy with your central area or someone will park their tent in it.
- Make the camp comfy. It's great fun to get back to camp for some dinner after a hard day Festivalling to relax a while, eat and then get glammed up for a big night out.
- Tie a flag, some bunting or a balloon to your tent so you can spot it in a sea of others.
- Make sure you have enough dry, clean clothes with you – even if you can't wash yourself too easily it's nice to have a clean pair of pants or two.
- Take lots of photos – your friends have never looked so happy and healthy or silly.
- Don't keep all your money in one place.
- Don't stay out in the sun too long. Wear sun screen and drink loads of water.
- Tie some ribbon on to a small torch and wear it round your neck for finding your tent/the loo/the last of the beers in the dark.
- Always take some fancy clothes to dress up in. Why not have a group theme? Get carried away – dressing up is the only way to go at festivals, you'll have so much more fun and meet so many more people.

Festival essentials

Tickets

Wheelbarrow or something to get your stuff from the car to where you're camping

Something to make your tent stand out so you can find it

More dressing-up stuff

Condoms and painkillers

Earplugs and eye mask

Money

Lots of friends

Packing

Clothes

- For the girls, nighties are great in the summer because you'll look glamorous at camp – and you never know who you might meet. Pyjamas and thick socks are a must when it's chilly (not quite so glamorous, but warm).
- For the boys, big coats are great for fitting in a lady or two and big scarves are essential to lasso them in with.
- For the kids, take lots of clothes and lots of socks as they seem to go through them at a rate of knots. Layer them up so they can peel off or on when they get hot or cold.
- For all campers alike, a big blanket makes a great coat. Wrap up tightly around the campfire and make the most of the stored-in warmth by taking it to bed with you.

Other stuff

A large plastic bucket is useful for many things:

- As a fridge – fill with cold water, put the things you want to keep cool in waterproof wrapping and put them in the bucket. Place the bucket in a cool spot or a stream (tied to something!).
- To put wet shoes and sandy clothes in.
- For stand-up washes.
- As storage for water next to the campfire in case of an emergency.
- To wash your hair in.
- To collect anything you wish to gather, from nettles to fish to wood to shells to moons.*

A tarpaulin or a big sheet of plastic is invaluable when you're camping:

- To shelter you and your stuff from rain or shine.
- To sit on.
- To mark out and save camp space for your friends.
- To cut a hole in the middle of and wear as a raincoat.

Pack your crockery and clothes in plastic or wooden boxes – these can double up as tables or store cupboards in your camp kitchen. At home, it's a good idea to box together all your camping china, crockery and old pans so that they're ready and waiting for your next trip. And always take enough water.

Packing the car

- Put the biggest and heaviest things in first.
- Put your duvets and pillows on the back seat to make a comfy bed for mid-journey snoozing.
- Put the crockery and food boxes within easy reach so when you stop on the way you can have a picnic.
- Put the tent, mallet and torch in last as they will be the first things out.
- And always have the red wine, brandy or beer handy.

*available only to hippies.

Big kids

- Have a sing-off. See who can sing along the loudest to whatever's playing on the radio.
- Make up silly stories about people in other cars.
- Play pants! You must answer only 'pants!' to any question you are asked. For example: 'Where are we going today?' 'Pants!' if you laugh, you're out and it's the next person's turn. The winner is the person who can carry on the longest without laughing and the prize is to choose a word to replace 'pants!' for the next game.
- Play I-spy.
- Do the crossword.
- Knit a scarf.
- Read (as long as you don't get car sick).
- Play film-/rock-star alphabet. One person names a film or rock star. The next person has to name another star beginning with the last letter of the previous star and so on and so on until you get bored.
- Have a kip (unless you're driving) – you'll get there quicker.
- Be a map nerd like Tess.
- Play word association. One person says a word. The next person says a new word which is associated with the previous word. The next person says a word associated with that word and so on and so on. For example: camping – fire – flames – phoenix – beast – tiger – grrrr – angry – happy – campers.

Little kids

- Teach them to map-read or give them directions to where you're going so they can help you navigate and be a map nerd like Tess.
- Make up a story or put on a story tape.
- Pack lots of healthy snacks – they can't make as much noise with their mouths full.
- Play the silent game – see who can stay silent the longest. The winner gets a prize – and if you're really lucky they might all fall asleep trying.
- When you're at the end of your tether and your little angels won't simmer down, stop at an open space or friendly field. Let them run a round for a bit, give them some carbohydrates, wait a while and put them back in the car. Hopefully after about five minutes you'll have a car full of snoring angels.
- And if all else fails bribery and corruption work well . . .
- Use sweets to get them to behave. Set a time limit and every thirty minutes or so hand out a round of sweets and let them know that they will only get their next sweet if they behave (this works well for naughty adults too).
- Buy some cheap little prizes – for example, a comic, toy car, puzzle, etc. – and wrap them into little presents. Then decide on a distance limit of, say, fifty miles or so. If they have behaved themselves after this distance (which they invariably do) they receive a prize. The kids are happy and occupied till the next prize.

setting up camp

Setting up camp

Depending on who you're with and where you're camping, the process of choosing where you're going to pitch your tent can be either a complete breeze or a diplomatic nightmare.

An efficiently run camp ground with your family is a million miles away from letting a gaggle of mates loose on a maze of fields come festival season and even further away from being completely out in the wilds. Here are a few things to think about when you are setting up your camp and to make your stay in the countryside a happy one.

When you arrive

The first thing to do when you arrive is to put the kettle on so by the time you have finished putting your tent up, tea will be up.

Plan to arrive in daylight. This way you will have the advantage of sight. If you arrive while it's still light you'll be able to work out where the sun sets and rises and choose which way to face your front door. Do you like shade in the morning for a slow rise for breakfast, or do you need that extra push of light streaming in to your tent to get you out of bed? Or perhaps you would like to view the setting sun from your bed.

But don't worry: if, come the end of work on a Friday night, you are itching to get away from it all and it's dark by the time you arrive at your destination, just have a torch or even better a head torch at the ready and be prepared to move things around a little come the morning.

Pitching your tent

When you are pitching your tent don't forget to think about what the weather might do. Yes, we British love our weather – after all, it gives us something to talk about. The chances are that you'll be camping when the forecast is good. But the good old British weather invariably doesn't do what it's supposed to so always be prepared.

Remember that old phrase 'high and dry'. Low areas can be pockets for cold air and collect rain like a sponge, so on rainy nights pitch your tent higher up or it might not be waterproof for long. Higher ground is good but you're then exposed to wind, so use hedges and other natural windbreaks to your advantage. Don't camp under trees in strong winds – you don't want branches crashing down on you. That said, trees provide excellent refuge for shade seekers when those hot, sunny days are just too much. Bliss!

It's lovely to camp near a stream, river or the sea; the sound of the water is so relaxing and helps to filter out any unwanted noise. However, waterside pitches do pose some potential hazards.

Be sure it's not going to pelt down with rain if you're planning to camp near a river – you could wake to find the riverbanks burst and your tent on its way to the sea!

If you're lucky enough to be camping or sleeping on a beach, choose a spot well above the shoreline or you may end up going for an unplanned moonlit swim. You can usually tell where the shoreline is by the line of flotsam and jetsam (seaweed and other bits and pieces) on the beach.

Lightning strikes the highest object in an area, so don't put your tent under the tallest tree in the forest and don't camp in the middle of an open field.

A final personal word of warning from Tess and Karn: if you find yourself driving around in the dark, desperately looking for somewhere to camp, and end up having to pitch your tent for a not so romantic night's camping in a car park, just be ready for when the warden appears and sternly asks you to move on.

Once you've chosen your spot
- Look for a nice expanse of flattish ground clear of tree roots.
- Clear the site of stones and sharp sticks or you will regret it later, à la 'the princess and the pea'.
- If you do have a sloping site make your bed with the pillows at the top of the hill so your blood runs to your feet, not your head.
- Be careful not to park your tent over a wasps' or ants' nest (we know from bitter experience that wasps can nest in holes in the ground).

Other things to consider
- If campfires are permitted, where is the wood pile and is there already a fire pit?
- Do you want neighbours or not?
- Where are the toilets, if any? It's no fun to have your camp on the main highway to the loos.
- Where is the water tap?
- Where do you park your car?
- Where do you put the rubbish?
- Are there any noisy kids (if you don't have any)?
- Are there any noisy kids for my noisy kids to play with (if you do)?
- Remember that it's fun! It's like building yourself a new house, or playing at being a kid again. Get creative and enjoy it.

Laying out your site

If there is just one tent to put up, then it's pretty simple: 'oh, that looks nice; the sun rises over there and I'd love that view in the morning. Let's camp there!'

Camping in a group makes it a bit trickier to organise the pitch. Inevitably everyone has their own idea of how things should be done, so some tact and negotiation skills can often come in handy.

A circle of tents is the traditional layout and, to our minds, is the best way to begin with, ideally with a campfire or other focal point at its heart. There's something very special about a circle of tents. It's so lovely to wake up to a new dawn, tiptoe out of your tent, put the kettle on and see sleepy faces emerge from their tents. As the night falls you can watch everyone sat around the roaring campfire, sharing stories into the small hours as one by one they slip off to their boudoirs.

You do need to ensure that the tents aren't too close to the fire (if you're allowed one) and check the wind direction so no one gets smoke billowing into their tent – though this seems to be unavoidable, however hard we try.

If you can't have a fire make a communal seating area, with candles and even flowers if you're feeling decorative. You could also make or take a shelter with you to put over the communal area, for shade or protection from the rain. Gazebos are very cheap but it's probably just as easy and more fun to make yourself a shelter with some tarpaulin. But if you have got a fire please don't put your gazebo over the top of it.

Take sheepskins and lay them over plastic matting; they make wonderful insulators for your posterior and are really comfy and warm.

Eating is the favourite camping pastime, so put the camp kitchen, if you're having one, in or near the circle if you can as it's always a hive of activity. Try to make this a shaded spot away from the heat of the fire.

It's not always possible to create the perfect camping circle. Don't worry if you can't – the main thing is to try to create a sociable camp, with all the tents facing towards the fire or communal area. Don't pitch a tent with its door facing the back of another tent and be sure to leave enough space between tents for a restful night's sleep. Tent walls aren't snore-proof, giggle-proof or indeed 'any other sort of noise you may care to make'-proof.

If you or one of your gang has a big tent, a tipi or bell tent with a big living area, a good idea is to position it near the middle of camp to be used as a living room, kitchen or poker den.

Likewise, if you or one of your gang has a camper-van or motor home, try to park it with its door facing into camp so it can be used to everyone's advantage. Some have awnings, which can provide shelter or shade; if yours doesn't, one can easily be fashioned by tying a tarpaulin to the sides of the camper and using poles or long sticks as props. The camp kitchen can be set up underneath and everyone gets to use the campers' facilities too.

Setting up your tent

Have your mallet and pegs to hand and use the instructions provided.

Get everyone to help each other. Or just get the others to set up the tents while you find the brandy and sort out the food.

Diagonal wrinkles in the floor inside your tent could indicate that you've stretched it too tightly in one direction – check for these while you're putting up the tent.

It's no mean feat to pitch a tent in windy conditions – a tent with no poles is essentially a great big kite. Gather some stones, logs or anything else heavy that you have to hand to hold down the tent and fly sheet. Grab some friends to help you. Stake the tent at one corner as a security measure in case of sudden gusts. Thread the poles through one at a time, staking as you go, and use your guy ropes for extra stability.

Inside your tent

We know this sounds geeky but keeping your tent organised from the outset makes camping life so much more pleasant. Weirdly, Tess is obsessively tidy when camping but at home it's quite a different story.

- Keep the sleeping area free from muddy boots and muddy boys.
- If you have a porch in your tent, put the food in there; if not, keep the food at the doorway.
- Use your dustpan and brush to sweep out leaves, dirt, sand and spiders.
- Keep a camp lamp near the door inside your tent. Camp lamps are great and are widely available at camp shops. Alternatively, you can use candles but must always blow them out when you leave the tent or slip off to dreamland. To make your own camp lamp, put some sand into a jam jar (so the heat doesn't melt your groundsheet) then place a tea-light on the sand. Make a handle out of wire and you have the perfect cheap, easy and pretty camp light.
- Use s-hooks to hang things from your tent roof. Hang your torch within arm's reach of your bed.
- Zip up your tent when the sun starts to set in order to keep in the day's warmth and avoid condensation as the temperature drops.
- That old bit of carpet that's been in your car boot can be used as your tent's doormat.

Getting a good night's sleep

Bedtime is heavenly when you're camping. Sleeping under the stars, listening to the murmur of your neighbours, the pitter-patter of rain or the gentle lapping of water can all lull you off into a deep, luxurious sleep . . . But only if you're comfy.

Why make do with an old, thin, nylon sleeping-bag when it requires just a little extra effort to take your duvet, sheets, sheepskins, pillows and blankets and have yourself the best bed ever? Believe us, it's worth it – if you get a good night's sleep you wake up refreshed, and you feel so smug in your big delicious bed. We have an ongoing challenge to see who can make the comfiest bed.

Another great thing about making super-comfy beds is that you can pull them outside in the morning and lie in with the best view in the world.

- For extra luxury wrap up your toasty warm hot-water bottle with your duvet half an hour before you go to bed.
- Tuck a sheepskin under your sheets for some added comfort and warmth.
- If you don't like the idea of taking your duvet, zip two sleeping bags together and steal someone else's warmth.
- Weather permitting, air your bed during the day.

Come night time, just pop on your nightie or jim jams. Climb into your super-cosy camping bed and dream of tomorrow's delights.

The campfire

A campfire is for so much more than just cooking and warmth. There's the scent of wood smoke that stays in your hair for days, the warm glow that keeps you toasty all night long under the stars, the unique opportunity to enjoy your friends with no distractions and the trance we all seem to fall into as we stare at the flickering flames. All sense of time slips away as we share secrets, sing songs and tell bad jokes, sip a hot toddy or two and share a baked chocolate banana with a loved one while sitting around a crackling fire after a long, hard day of having fun.

Campfire ingredients

You're going to need three types of wood to get the fire going. This is a great opportunity to delegate to those people who would otherwise get under your feet – i.e., children, partners and friends, basically everyone – while you go and raid the chocolate supply. Or you could all go exploring together and collect wood on the way back to camp.

Tinder

You need something that catches fire easily. Strips of paper, wood shavings, bark, pine needles, dry grass . . . A couple of handfuls of anything small and flammable are what's needed. Alternatively have a go at making fuzz sticks. Get a load of sticks and shred the top of each one, leaving the shredded pieces attached – so they look like model palm trees. Prop the fuzz sticks upright in among the kindling. Firelighters are also an option.

Kindling

You'll need an armful. Dry twigs are best. Most people look on the floor for firewood but in fact what's on the ground tends to be wet, so look for small dead branches up in the trees (don't go sawing up or cutting down healthy, living trees, though). You can also make kindling by cutting up bigger logs with an axe or saw.

Fuel

Lastly you'll need the fuel that's going to keep you warm. Good campsites provide wood but if necessary you can usually buy it locally too. Or you can gather your own – in which case you're looking for big logs and large pieces of wood, preferably dry. Don't bother with green, live wood; this is full of moisture and won't burn. Hardwoods such as ash, oak, birch, beech and sweet chestnut are best, because they burn more slowly so are better for cooking over. Softwoods such as pine, hawthorn and poplar burn fast but are fine for making a cup of tea. Try to take just the amount you need – usually about as much as you can carry; you can always go back for more if necessary – and from as wide an area as possible, as deadwood often provides a home for woodland critters that are an important part of the ecosystem.

Optional extras

Firelighters, Blankets, Big log to sit on, Someone to attract smoke, Something to sup, Camp stories/songs

Beech wood fires are bright and clear,
If the logs are kept a year.
Chestnut's only good, they say,
If for long it's laid away.
Birch and fir logs burn too fast,
Blaze up bright and do not last.
Elm wood burns like churchyard mould,
Even the very flames are cold.
Poplar gives a bitter smoke,
Fills your eyes and makes you choke.
Apple wood will scent your room
With an incense like perfume.
Oak and maple, if dry and old,
Keep away the winter cold.
But ash wood wet and ash wood dry,
A king shall warm his slippers by.

Let's build a fire

- Before choosing where to build the fire, check which way the wind is blowing in relation to your tent: you want a home to sleep in tonight.
- If there isn't a fire pit already there, cut away a slice of earth and grass. You can replace it later so no one will ever know that you built a campfire.
- Start off with a small, loose pile of tinder, making sure you allow space for air to feed the fire. Next, build a small pyramid of kindling around the pile of tinder. Try to stay focused at this point – remember, a small pyramid; resist the temptation to recreate one of the seven wonders of the world.
- Light the tinder with a match. Add more kindling, still keeping the pyramid shape.
- As the fire grows in strength, gradually add increasingly larger sticks and then logs.
- Leave enough space between them for the fire to breathe and be careful not to smother the fire by adding all your fuel at once.
- If the fire is struggling, crouch down low and blow gently at it from the side to encourage the flames. Keep an eye on the fire and add more fuel when it dies down.
- Finally, find a long, skinny stick. Place a marshmallow on the end of the stick and roast it over the fire you have just built, bathing in the warmth and glory that a fire brings.

Campfire safety

- A fire is one of the nicest things to have when camping but obviously care must be taken to prevent it spreading out of control. Surrounding the fire with logs or large stones can help to contain it.
- Never use petrol, lighter fluid, aerosol cans or gas cylinders to help ignite a fire. If your wood is too wet to burn, have an early night or buy some dry wood.
- Remember that wood, petrol and people burn well, so be careful what you put near the fire.
- Keep a supply of water, soil or sand nearby with which to put out the fire when you go to bed (or, worst-case scenario, for use in a tent-on-fire emergency). Don't assume that the fire will go out on its own. Pour lots of water (or soil or sand) over the embers to completely extinguish them – do watch out for the cloud of smoke this will cause.
- Always make sure the ashes are cold when you leave the fire. If necessary, stir the wet embers and cover with more water.
- In the event of your clothing catching fire, roll around on the ground until the fire goes out.
- Even better, politely ask a friend to fetch a blanket to wrap you in and smother the flames.
- Never put dressings on burns. Run cold water on the burn until you can't feel pain any more. For serious burns always seek medical attention. For very small burns a dab of lavender essential oil is like magic.

The camp kitchen

Your camp's kitchen space can be a basic set-up at the doorway of your tent or something as elaborate as a separate, sheltered area containing a cooker, fridge and dishwasher (gas stove, icebox and husband). We're not suggesting that you need anything grand, but if you're camping in a group it makes sense to allocate a space for all things food.

Choose a place free of dry twigs and leaves, which may catch fire from your stove, and preferably away from direct sunlight too. You can make a simple tarpaulin shelter or buy a cheap garden gazebo. Wherever you put your kitchen space, never use your stove inside your tent. Turn it off when it's not in use and keep gas canisters outside and matches in a waterproof container.

If you use plastic stacking boxes for transporting your supplies these can be swiftly upturned for use as a food-preparation area. It's a good idea to bring at least a couple of these waterproof crates to store your food in; ones with lids are especially useful for stopping any creepy crawlies or hungry sheep nosing around in your supplies. You can also keep food in sealed plastic bags, put up high so nothing can get at them.

Ideally keep your perishables cool in an icebox in the shade. Cartons of frozen juice work almost as well as icepacks in your cooler. Remember that a bucket filled with cold water can be used instead of a proper icebox (see page 56).

We usually sit to eat either on sheepskin rugs set out on the floor or on large logs if there are any nearby. Foldaway tables and chairs and deckchairs can all be bought quite cheaply from most camping shops. A couple of old tables with the legs lopped off halfway make great banqueting tables, with cushions for chairs, and we have been known to really go to town, with white linen tablecloths, candlesticks and wildflowers for a big birthday feast.

Washing up

When it comes to the washing up, the first rule is to delegate. If that fails, here are some handy tips:

- Keep your kitchen area clean and try to do the washing up straight away or you'll attract unwanted creepy crawlies and furry friends.
- When you've finished cooking, put a big pan or kettle of water on the stove or campfire before you eat so that there is hot water ready for you to wash up with afterwards.
- Scrape food debris from your plates into the bin before you wash up; there will be less mess and the water you later discard won't attract beasties.
- Remove stuck-on food from pans by boiling some water in them. Always put hot water in the scrambled-egg pan as soon as you've emptied it – or, better still, use a non-stick pan.
- Always use biodegradable washing-up liquid or just straight water.
- Wait until the used water cools before disposing of it and throw over a wide area away from your camp. This way you won't kill the flora and fauna with your hot soapy water.

The powder room

How to dig la toilette

In wild areas you won't have the luxury of facilities, so this may be your only option. To make an al fresco loo you will need:

A trowel or spade
Loo roll
A couple of recycled plastic bags
Organic wet wipes

- Select a secluded spot with some natural screening at least seventy steps away from any water source and preferably downwind from camp. Beneath a tree is perfect, though decomposition of your waste will be quicker in a sunny spot. Wherever it is, watch out for stinging nettles.
- Dig a small hole, fifteen to twenty centimetres deep and about the length from your elbow to your fingertips.
- You can bury unscented, un-dyed toilet paper but it really is better to put it in a bin, so tie a plastic bag securely near the loo use as one. (Ladies, please don't bury your sanitary stuff; animals will just dig it up again. It should be put in a plastic bag and disposed of responsibly.)
- Tie the loo roll close by.
- If there is not a nearby water source for hand-washing, take some organic wet wipes.
- If there are only a few of you, you can each dig your own loos as necessary; otherwise use leaves or soil to cover your doings so they don't offend the next person.
- Remember to replace the earth into the hole before you leave camp and be sure to take all your rubbish away with you.

See – that wasn't so traumatic, was it?

Keeping clean

When camping a bit of dirt won't hurt but a shower can be a real luxury. At busy campsites and festivals, time your shower to avoid the queues: go in the early afternoon or late evening; if you're an early riser you could try very early morning. Failing all else, wet wipes are invaluable for in-between-shower days. When visiting the shower, flip-flops are the best choice of footwear as it's impossible to put socks on damp feet.

If you're in the wilds you could use a shower bag. This is a large plastic bag with a spout that you fill with water and leave out to let the sun do its good work. When the water has warmed up you simply hang the bag in a tree and enjoy your shower. Do remember to use biodegradable cleansing products that won't damage the environment.

Alternatively, just have a water fight using recycled washing-up liquid bottles – you don't get as clean but it's more fun.

Another great trick is to run a small towel under cold water then squeeze it out. Use it for stand-up washes, dirty children, menopausal hot-flush mums, headaches and on hot days to cool you down.

Or just find the nearest lido/swimming pool/lake or sea and have a wash there.

Camp health and safety tips

- Watch out for guy ropes and don't leave tent pegs sticking out to stub your toes on. If you can't avoid having something sticking out, try to cover it with a bit of foam and tape.
- Keep gas canisters upright at all times and store outside, well away from campfires.
- Store food in a cool place to avoid food poisoning.
- Never use your stove in a tent or a confined area.
- Always pack a first-aid kit.
- Wear sunscreen – you can get burnt even on overcast days.
- Be careful around water and keep an eye on your children – everyone should know how to swim.
- Put your rubbish in your car at night. There's nothing worse than spending the morning cleaning up after a fox's dinner when you're meant to be on the beach catching some rays.
- Always take your rubbish home with you and recycle where possible.
- Be nice to spiders: think of them as your friends.
- Keep a clean camp or the ants will.

The dreaded midge

As kids growing up in the wilds of Wales we were covered in calamine lotion for the majority of our summers. The problem was that midges shared our love of playing in the river so we just had to accept the bites as something that came with the territory.

Midges bite early in the morning and one or two hours after sunset. They're attracted to strong perfumes and bright or dark colours so go natural and wear white. Just like their vampire ancestors, they hate garlic so eat lots for tea. Light some citronella candles and wear coconut-scented sunscreen as they don't like the smell of either. Lastly, midges hate smoke so try sitting near the campfire. Hopefully by this point your human friends won't have deserted you!

There's no place like home . . .

Making your camp a home

Although it's not for everyone (boys), making your camp beautiful, even if only for a short stay is lovely and great fun to do. So bring a vase and go for a walk and pick some wildflowers from the hedgerows. There are lots of protected species so pick only common flowers (see Wild World section, page 218) and then only if there will be plenty left for others to enjoy. Boys, we do promise that getting up one morning to go picking wildflowers for your lady will earn you about a million brownie points.

Tablecloths are great for hiding ugly foldaway tables and, being no longer de rigueur in our homes, can be picked up very cheaply from charity shops and car-boot sales. Also look out for cheap pretty china or second-hand glasses rather than using their paper or plastic counterparts.

Get creative and make yourself some camping furniture.

Ribbons, flags and bunting can all beautify your camp area as well as help you to spot your home in a sea of others at festivals and large campsites. This also works well for kids who've strayed too far from home and have difficulty spotting which tent is theirs.

Why not take a glitter ball to hang in the trees and sparkle sunlight around? They keep little babies mesmerised for hours. Pebbles are great for making fairy rings and pathways. Collect some large stones for resting hot pans on.

Tea-lights and candles bring a bit of romance to camp. Tell the kids you've caught a flock of fireflies by making twinkling bean-can holders: punch holes in the sides, attach some wire for a handle, put a tea-light inside and hang in the trees. Or make lots of jam jar tea-light holders (see page 69) to be dotted around or simply arrange a load of different-sized candles on a tray. Take candelabras or candlesticks and have them as a table centrepiece. These are great if you're not allowed a fire and can easily be found at junk shops and flea markets.

Build a shelter

If your tarpaulin doesn't have ready-made holes but you'd like to attach a rope to it, rather than making your own holes (which will tear the sheet) find a smallish smooth stone to use as an anchor: wrap it in the corner of the sheet and tie your rope around it, trapping the stone within the tarp.

If there are no handy tree branches, and you're not going to tie your rope to a car or camper-van, you will need to find something to attach the other end to. If you can find a Y-shaped branch, push the forked end into the ground and tie the rope to the top. Alternatively, tie the rope to a stick, dig a hole, secure the stick in the walls of the hole and fill in the hole, or even just tie the rope to a stick, put the stick on the ground and place a large rock on top.

'Have you noticed that everything an Indian does is in a circle? That is because the power of the world always works in circles. The sky is round and so is the earth. The wind, in its greatest power whirls. Birds make their nests in circles; the sun comes forth and goes down again in a circle, the moon does the same and both are round. Even the seasons form a great circle in their changing, and always come back again to where they were. The life of man is a circle from childhood to childhood. Our tipis are round like the nests of birds and these were always set in a circle, a nest of many nests where the great spirit meant for us to hatch our children.'

Black Elk, 1930
Black Elk belonged to the Oglala division of the Teton Dakota, one of the most powerful branches of the Siouan family.

Camping food

One of camping's simplest pleasures is cooking and eating outside. Food tastes incredible when eaten outdoors; fresh air seems somehow to clean the palette and intensify the flavours – even more so if there is salt around (yet another good reason to camp near the beach). If you're lucky enough to be cooking on a campfire you'll find the tastes heightened even further. The delicate, wood-smoked flavours are out of this world and it's such a pleasure to cook up a feast on glowing hot coals, surrounded by your loved ones laughing and chattering away. The wood ash blown in from the fire is often the secret ingredient in many of our recipes! When the food is ready, the fire is stoked and everyone gathers around, perching on logs or sitting on the floor. Steaming foil-wrapped presents, fresh from the fire, are passed around and it feels like Christmas. You dig out the sweet, succulent flesh of baked salmon, the edges deliciously caramelised, and there's fluffy baked potatoes on the side to soak up the lovely lemony basil juices . . . Yum.

But all is not lost if you can't have a campfire: you can still create amazing culinary delights on your camp stove or portable barbecue. There is no reason why food shouldn't be as good at camp as it is at home, if not better, and there's certainly no reason to cook the traditional camping fare of sausage and beans every night (although that's not to say that these things aren't fantastic every now and then). With just a little planning you can make amazingly tasty, simple food that is a delight to eat, healthy and fun to cook.

We love food! When we go camping food is always the hottest topic of conversation. Many a happy day has been spent discussing, planning, hunting and gathering our favourite ingredients. If we're at camp, lunch can be a simple affair – a salad or some snackette, usually devised by Tess. If we're out having fun somewhere, we might take a picnic, cook up some fresh fish on the beach, or even grab hot, fat pasties tucked into paper-bag plates, and all the while we'll be probably be thinking about, talking about and planning the next food extravaganza.

We try to buy local, organic or pesticide-free food where possible and to eat as seasonally as we can. This is good not only for us and our environment but also for the small, independent food producers. By supporting local grocery stores, fishmongers and butchers in the area where you're staying you are helping to ensure that they will be there

the next time you visit. It's truly amazing, the variety of ingredients that you can get from farm shops, pick-your-owns, farmers markets, roadside stalls and specialist shops. Aside from being a good excuse to explore the area and meet some of the colourful locals, it's brilliant fun to try out different foods, from samphire in Norfolk to clotted cream in Devon with all those cheeses, meats, fresh fish and other local specialties in between.

We also love to do a bit of foraging for wild food. As it satisfies the hunter-gatherer in us and nothing tastes better than something that's freshly picked and totally free.

All of our recipes have been invented, discovered, collected and borrowed by us, our friends and our families throughout our camping lives. Most are quite flexible, so, for example, cow's milk can easily be substituted for soya, goat's or rice milk and plain flour for spelt or gluten-free, etc. Our aim is to try to show how easy it is to make scrumptious food and to inspire you to get creative in your camp kitchen. Don't altogether forget the classic camping dishes, but do remember that it's easy to roast a fish with a few fresh herbs, or to make a beautiful soup, a delicious pot roast or an Indian feast complete with chapattis cooked on a spade.

Finally, don't forget you that one of the best things about camping has to be the fact that, having expended so much energy having fun, you can spoil yourself with a bit of what you fancy. So go on, treat yourself, have another helping of our camping tiramisu.

What's in season when?

Food tastes best when it's in season because that is when it is naturally ready to be eaten. The following poem might help you when you're out and about:

Roots and sprouts available be, throughout Jan and February.
Leeks, cauliflower and cabbage, too, can be enjoyed ere winter's through.
Then colours come with March's thaw, rhubarb, carrots (and beets from store).

But April's menus are a riddle, as stored crops run out in the middle;
Mere salads must your table dress, with lettuces and watercress.

May can be warm, but it is cruel; few things grow this month, as a rule.
But then at last some lunch appears: new potatoes and asparagus spears!
Rejoice therefore and clap your hands; now is the time to slaughter lambs!

In June, the veg are in full swing, and so are some fruits, including:
Blackcurrants, cherries and tomatoes (they are a fruit, like avocados).
Berries too are on the loose, the early ones, both straw and goose.

In summer, veg are hard to miss, thanks to photosynthesis:
Fennel, herbs, beans green and broad, carrots can again be stored,
Peppers, courgettes, nice and chewy, time to make some ratatouille!

Then tree fruit with September comes (that means apples, pears and plums.)
Soon purple things are also seen: red cabbage, beets and aubergine.
And now's the time, in case you wondered, that onions and spuds are keenly plundered.

The growing season's nearly over, when marrow's plucked around October,
Although this month is also big in apples, pears and fresh-picked fig.

By Guy Fawkes' night the frost is freed, but that won't stop the hearty swede.
Parsnips, too, the soils expel, some cabbages and leeks as well.
They'll be needed, just remember, as bugger all grows in December.

Leo Benedictus

And here is a little list of our own:
   April – salmon, sea trout, wild garlic
   May – sea bass, sardines, sorrel
   June – salmon, mackerel, crab, elderflower
   July – trout, pilchard, fennel, sage
   August – skate, whitebait, samphire
   September – brown trout, mussels, sea bass, blackberries, damsons, sweet chestnuts
   October – oysters, mussels, squash, elderberries, hazelnuts

Food essentials

The following food items are things that we would never leave home without:

Salt mill (filled with sea salt)

Pepper mill

Olive oil

Tamari (like soy sauce only better)

Teabags (regular tea and herb teas)

A pint of milk (you can always get more fresh milk)

Fresh coffee

Honey or sugar

Bread and butter

Oat flakes and millet flakes (Tess can't be without her millet porridge)

Lemons

Bullion or stock cubes

Seeds (perfect for sprinkling on salads, baked potatoes, porridge, etc., and also good for you)

Spices and herbs

Brandy (purely medicinal, of course)

Mustard, eggs, bacon, tomato ketchup, beans

Chocolate

Different ways of cooking

On a campfire

Cooking on campfire is really easy. The fire is ready to cook on when all the wood has turned white and the flames have died down. At this point you will get an even heat and the flames won't burn your food.

The simplest way to cook on your fire is to find three or four big damp logs – or rocks, if no logs can be found (don't use either flint, which will explode, or slate, which will fall apart), arrange them around the fire, and then rest the grill on top.

When you build your fire remember to make some spaces so your foil-wrapped dinner parcels can easily be tucked in for roasting.

If you want a cooking space separate from your campfire, simply use damp logs or stones to make a U shape coming off the main fire. Rake the hot coals into this and put the grill on top.

To construct a basic cooking crane, drive two sturdy forked sticks (about four or five centimetres in diameter) into the ground either side of the fire, place a hardwood stick across the top and a couple of S-hooks on that. Hang your kettle from the hooks and Bob's your uncle: hot water for all to enjoy.

If you are going to the beach for the day and/or evening it's worth making a quick fire to cook on. Make a round hollow in the sand, about fifty or sixty centimetres across and thirty centimetres deep and place stones evenly around it (the windier it is, the more stones you will need). Build your fire inside the hollow and when it's ready to cook on rest the grill over the top.

Barbecues

Compact barbecues are very reasonably priced and brilliant to take camping with you – especially if you already have one hanging about in the back garden. Even if your chosen campsite has barbecue facilities, having your own in the boot of your car is really useful for beach picnics and the like. Disposable barbecues are also very handy and readily available.

Dad's cast-iron plate barbecue

Papa Carr was a legendary barbecue maker. He had a big, heavy cast-iron plate that he would always put in the back of the Land Rover to take on every camping trip. It seemed crazy to lug this huge thing around, but it was actually well worth it. The Carr family would have the best food on the campsite. Tess's mum would make huge stacks of Scotch pancakes for breakfast so the Carr kids had no trouble at all making friends. So if you come across a cast-iron plate, keep it as they make fantastic barbecues.

Stoves

A good stove is definitely an essential item when camping, especially if you can't have a campfire. In fact, we take ours even when we can have a fire, as it's always ready for that essential first cuppa in the morning, if the fire is out or it's raining. We both have simple gas stoves with two burners and a little grill; we got ours second-hand but they are cheap to buy and you can get the gas bottles refilled easily at camping shops.

Other ways

If you want to try baking at camp, you could use a Dutch oven. This is a small, cast-iron cauldron with legs and a lid, in which you can bake almost anything. They're great but very heavy and so not easily portable. You could make yourself a homemade biscuit-tin oven, or take a metal dustbin and give a roast dinner a go. Alternatively simply use sticks to make our simple biscuit recipe (see page 169).

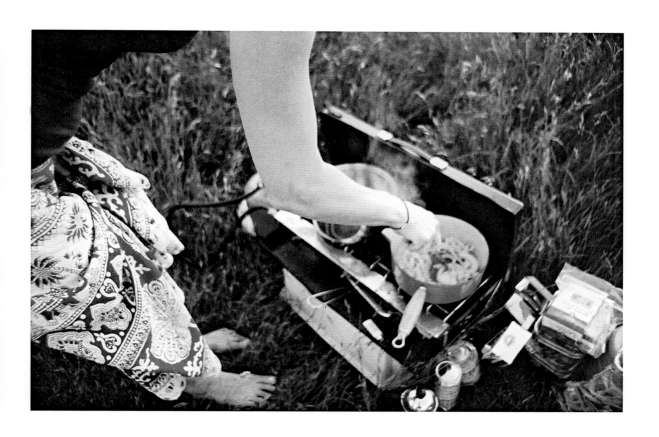

Food to make before you go

It's a real treat to arrive at camp and eat something homemade with your well-deserved 'I managed to get the tent up in record time' cup of tea. We like to bake before we go camping because it's quite tricky to do once you're there. We also like to take along a few things that help us with making meals during our trip. We're not suggesting that you make everything listed; we usually just bake one thing and make up a jar of something if we have time.

Lady Isla's polenta bread

Our friend and Karn's sister, the lovely Isla, discovered this recipe when she stayed on an ashram in Australia. Wrap the bread in a clean tea towel or greaseproof paper tied up with string to take with you; it's perfect with some hot soup or toasted with some local cheese for the first night under the stars. The recipe is very adaptable so ingredients can easily be substituted. Try making it with goats' cheese, thyme and caramelised red onion; pear and chocolate; or lemon and almond (replacing the flour with ground almonds and adding sugar to taste).

Makes 2 loaves

> 4 cups polenta
> 2 cups flour (you can use spelt, plain, brown rice or whatever you have to hand)
> 1 heaped teaspoon baking powder
> $\frac{1}{2}$ cup olive oil
> 5 cups milk (you can use soya or rice milk if you want)
> 1 cup Greek yoghurt
> 1 jar sundried tomatoes, drained and chopped
> 1 can pitted black olives, halved
> 1 can sweetcorn, drained
> Handful fresh rosemary, roughly chopped
> 1 pack feta cheese
> Salt and pepper

Preheat the oven to 170°c/325°f/gas mark 3. In a large bowl mix together the polenta, flour, baking powder, salt and pepper. In a separate bowl combine the oil, milk and yoghurt; the mixture may curdle but don't worry. Add to the dry ingredients and mix well. Stir in the tomatoes, olives, sweetcorn, rosemary and crumbled feta. The mixture should be quite runny – add more milk if it feels sticky. Grease and flour two loaf tins. Pour in the mixture and bake in the oven for 45 minutes or until the tops of the loaves are firm and golden brown. Turn out on to a wire rack, allow to cool, and try not to eat it all before you go camping.

Tamari and garlic toasted seeds

This is a brilliant snack, full of essential oils and other goodness. We always try to take a big jar when we go camping.

Choose your seeds – whatever you fancy, in any ratio: pumpkin, sunflower, sesame, linseed, etc.

Preheat the oven to 150°c/300°f/gas mark 2. Scatter the seeds on a roasting tray with a couple of freshly chopped garlic cloves and a good lug of tamari – enough to lightly cover the seeds. Roast in the oven until the seeds start popping, then remove and leave to cool. Break up the clusters that will have formed and pour into a jam jar or sealy bag to take with you.

Red-onion marmalade

This is perfect served with a good local cheese or to perk up fire-cooked sausages.

In a heavy-based sauté pan gently heat the olive oil. Add 4 or 5 roughly chopped red onions and a generous sprinkling of soft brown sugar. Fry over a very low heat, stirring occasionally, until soft and slightly caramelised. Be patient – the longer it takes the better it will be. When the edges of the onions have started to brown add 1 glass of red wine and 7 tablespoons of red-wine vinegar. Turn up the heat and cook until the liquid has reduced to a sticky jam. Remove from the heat, season to taste and leave to cool.

Store in a jam jar until you're ready to go camping.

Mama Carr's raspberry jam

This is the best raspberry jam in the whole world.

2.4kg (6lbs) fresh raspberries
2.4kg (6lbs) granulated or preserving sugar

Preheat the oven to 100°c. Place a saucer in the freezer. Set a big pan over a low heat and add the raspberries, stirring gently to draw out the juice. Meanwhile, warm the sugar in the oven, then carefully add to the raspberries. Let the sugar dissolve slowly, stirring occasionally. When the sugar is completely dissolved, bring to the boil and cook rapidly, stirring all the time to even out the temperature. After 5 to 10 minutes set aside and test to see if will set. Do this by dropping a little of the mixture on the saucer you've chilled then returning the saucer to the freezer for a few minutes. If after that time the jam doesn't part and wrinkle when you draw your finger through it, it needs to be boiled for longer. Repeat the process, boiling the jam for a few minutes more, until it sets on the saucer as described. Pour into warmed jars and leave to cool. Seal each jar with greaseproof paper and a lid. Take to every camp and taste the summer in every mouthful.

Pesto

Pesto is great at camp and once you've tried the homemade variety you'll never go back. You can make it before you go but it's also really easy to make at camp.

Kat's pesto

1 large plant or bunch of basil
Small handful pine nuts
Small handful grated parmesan
1 clove garlic
Good-quality olive oil
Black pepper

Toast the pine nuts in an un-oiled pan – watch carefully as they brown quickly! Finely chop or bash the nuts, basil and garlic. Grate the parmesan. Mix all together with some olive oil until your desired consistency. Season with plenty of black pepper.

Tess's pesto

For Tess's pesto simply add a handful of cashew nuts and a small handful of grated pecorino cheese along with the other ingredients.

Use your pesto to:
- Make fish with a pesto crust: – smother fillets or steaks of whatever fish you have (salmon works well) with some pesto, wrap in foil and bury in the hot coals.
- Stir through fresh pasta and serve with some grated parmesan.
- Make pesto, mozzarella and tomato sandwiches.
- Have pesto on toast.
- Add to your soup or drizzle some on as you serve it.
- Add some olive oil and use as a delicious salad dressing.
- Add a dollop to your fire-baked potatoes instead of butter.
- Brush some pesto on to your kebabs when you're roasting them on the fire or barbecue.
- Cook some lamb or chicken on the campfire or in a pan on your camp stove, spoon over the pesto for the last few minutes of cooking time.
- Grill any vegetables you choose on the barbecue, grill or fire and then smother in pesto to serve.
- For a twist on the traditional try replacing the basil with mint and coat lamb chops halfway through cooking.
- Try making different types of pesto – mint, parsley and toasted almonds, spinach and parmesan, coriander and pistachio.

Lizzie and Maddie's lemon spice cake
Kat's sister Lizzie and her friend Maddie used to make this nearly every week after school. It became a Heyes family tradition and has to be included here because it's so simple and amazingly scrumptious.

> 100g (4oz) wholemeal/plain/spelt (add a teaspoon of baking powder)
>   or self-raising flour
> 100g (4oz) oats
> 150g (6oz) butter
> 150g (6oz) soft brown sugar
> ¼ teaspoon nutmeg
> ½ teaspoon cinnamon
> 2 eggs
> Milk to mix
> Zest of 1 lemon
> 50g (2oz) walnuts or brazils or almonds

For the topping:
> 100g (4oz) soft brown sugar
> Juice of 1 lemon

Preheat the oven to 150°c/300°f/gas mark 2. Grease and line a 20cm/8in round tin. Cream together the butter and sugar and then beat in the eggs. Stir in the rest of ingredients. The mixture should be quite stiff but add a little milk if it feels too firm. Pour into the cake tin and bake for 30 minutes or until browned. Remove from the oven and leave to cool before wrapping in a clean tea towel or greaseproof paper. When you're ready to eat it, prod some holes in the cake with a fork, then mix together the lemon and sugar. Pour over the cake and eat immediately.

Mama Carr's cold tea loaf

This is the best camping fruit cake ever! Even Fred who doesn't like fruit cake loves this. We have it when we arrive at camp spread thick with butter, a nice cup of tea and a sit down; also this cake has no butter in it so it's fat free – until you spread butter all over it! This recipe makes three good-sized loaves.

900ml (1½ pints) strong tea (Yorkshire is best!)
300g (12oz) demerara or soft brown sugar
1.2kg (3lbs) mixed dried fruit and nuts (try raisins, currants, sultanas, apricots, dates, figs, glacé cherries, and a handful of chopped walnuts and almonds)
1 or 2 eggs, beaten
800g (2lbs) plain/spelt or self-raising flour
1 heaped teaspoon baking powder

Make the tea and leave to go cold. In a large bowl, add the sugar to the mixed dried fruit. Pour over the cold tea and mix well. Leave overnight if you can.

The next day, add the eggs, flour and baking powder. You may need to add a little milk or water for a sticky consistency.

Put into 3 greased bread tins (18cm/7in), hollowing out the centre a little. Cover with a foil hat, allowing plenty of head space for them to rise into. Bake in a moderate to low oven (120°c/248°f/gas mark 1) for approximately 3 hours. When ready, a knitting needle (you can use a knife here) should come out with no sticky stuff attached. Take off the foil 15 minutes before the end of the cooking time to brown off the tops. Leave to cool and pack in foil to take with you.

Kat's very chocolatey fudge brownies ... Yum yum yum

This is actually Kat's mum's recipe. They are totally foolproof and always impress.

175g (7oz) unsalted butter
6 very heaped tablespoons cocoa powder
4 eggs
350g (14oz) caster sugar/light brown sugar
1 teaspoon vanilla essence
100g (4oz) plain flour
350g (14oz) walnuts or pistachio nuts, chopped

Preheat the oven to 180°c/350°f/gas mark 4. Grease and line a square tin (24cm x 24cm approx) slowly melt the butter in a bowl over a pan of simmering water. When almost melted add the cocoa and stir to make a bitter chocolate sauce. Cool to lukewarm.

Whisk the eggs until foamy, then gradually beat in the sugar and vanilla to a creamy batter. Gently stir in the chocolate sauce; while still marbled fold in the flour and nuts, taking care not to over stir. Pour into the tin and bake in the oven for 25 minutes. Remove from the oven and leave to cool completely before cutting into slices. Pile into a cake tin, separating each layer with a slip of greaseproof paper. At camp simply hand round the tin and wait for the adoration.

Breakfasts

Waking up in camp is one of those magical moments. You're either the type who gets really excited and has to get up early (Tess, much to boyfriend Karn's annoyance), in which case you can put the kettle on and listen to your friends slowly stirring and the birds singing away, or you're the sort who's inclined to stay cosied up in bed (Kat and Fred) waiting for someone lovely to bring you a cuppa before you get up, in the meantime enjoying the banter that goes on from tent to tent. It's true what they say – breakfast is the most important meal of the day; and it's never more so than when you're camping, because you need your strength for all the fun you'll be having afterwards. We like to have a healthy, filling breakfast to give us energy (hence our obsession with porridge), but we also like to treat ourselves, especially on Sunday mornings, so we might have some fresh scotch pancakes, scrambled eggs and smoked salmon or even good old bacon butties . . . mmm.

Eggs

We love eggs. Why not have boiled eggs and soldiers? Just cut up the box to make egg cups and boil the eggs for exactly five minutes for the perfect egg. Make some toast on your new toasting fork (see page 117) and cut into soldiers.

For the best-ever scrambled eggs, just gently whisk two eggs per person – three for big boys – in a pan so the eggs are marbled-looking. Add a generous knob of butter and put over a low heat. Very gently stir the eggs while they cook, making sure they don't stick to the pan. When cooked add another knob of butter and some black pepper.

Some people seem to get their knickers in a twist about making poached eggs (Tess included until she encountered Kat's no-nonsense approach) but they are actually really easy:

Heat the water until you see tiny bubbles rising from the base of the pan; try to keep this temperature constant – you don't want a rolling boil but an occasional blip is fine.

Crack the eggs really gently into the water, one at a time, leaving a little space around each egg. Cook for about 3 to $3\frac{1}{2}$ minutes. If you have a lot to do you may need to cook them in two batches. Resist the temptation to poke them while they cook, which will just give you watery scrambled eggs for breakfast. Using a slotted spoon, scoop each egg on to buttered toast, then top with some smoked salmon, a grinding of pepper, a lemon squeeze and a smile.

Try Howy's (Tess's other brother) avocado on toast with a poached egg and bacon. It was his staple diet while camping his way round New Zealand. First, make some toast. Using a fork squash slices of avocado on to the toast, then drizzle with a little balsamic vinegar. Add a slice or two of crispy bacon and top off with a poached egg.

Millet and oat porridge with a bit of what you fancy

Ooooh porridge – we love porridge! People often turn their noses up at it but that's probably because they've never had it cooked properly, with just the right amount of love in it.

Feeds 6 hungry campers:
    3 cups organic rolled oats
    3 cups organic millet flakes
    Pinch salt (optional)
    6 cups milk – we use soya or rice milk as it tastes lighter.
    3 bananas (optional)
    2 handfuls of raisins or sultanas (optional)
    Whatever else you want to add
    6 spoonfuls of love

Other stuff you could add:
    Almonds
    Grated pears
    Dried apricots and figs
    Cardamom
    Cinnamon

Simply put all the ingredients into a saucepan and heat gently, stirring all the time (don't worry, it doesn't take long!). Add spoonfuls of love and keep stirring until the oats are cooked and the porridge is steaming. Add a little water or milk if it's too gloopy. We prefer it sticky but it's up to you. Serve in big bowls with a bit of what you fancy sprinkled on the top. Eat, feel happy and full.

To sprinkle on top
    Seeds (you can also put these in at the cooking stage)
    Honey
    Molasses
    Date syrup
    Soft dark brown sugar
    Milk
    Yoghurt
    Butter (if you're very naughty)
    Whisky (if you're in need of a kick)
    Maple syrup
    More love

Toast

Something as simple as a piece of toast can be the basis of many a camping meal but, without your trusty toaster or grill, how do you get the perfect slice? Making toast on the campfire is great fun and when Kat went to Australia she discovered the perfect way to make toast on the campfire using a homemade toasting fork.

Banana, peanut butter and honey on toast

Make some toast on the fire. Spread on some crunchy peanut butter, add sliced banana and drizzle over some local honey – repeat as required . . . mmm.

> ... other stuff to eat on toast:
> Tahini and honey
> Cheese and Marmite
> Soft cheese and raspberry jam
> Beans (got to get them in here somewhere!)

Big Ads's French toast with bacon and maple syrup

This french toast is also great with some fruit salad and dollops of thick Greek yoghurt.

> Bread (try with fruit bread or teacakes too)
> Good local back bacon
> 1 egg per person
> ½ teaspoon cinnamon
> ½ teaspoon nutmeg
> Maple syrup

Grill or fry the bacon till crispy. Meanwhile, using a fork, whisk the eggs with the ground cinnamon and nutmeg. Slice the bread and dip into the mixture until soaked right through. Fry until golden brown on both sides. Serve the french toast with the bacon and drizzle maple syrup on top.

How to make your own Aussie toasting fork
Simply take a metal coat hanger and bend into the shape shown. Pop your toast on the shelf you have created and hold over the campfire for toast cooked to perfection.

Jenny's (Tess's mum) hot Scotch pancakes

If hot summer days have turned your milk you've got the perfect excuse to make these little drops of heaven. They're smaller than normal pancakes so much easier to flip. You will need a flat griddle or large, heavy-based frying pan.

> 200g (8oz – about 2 cups) flour
> 1 level teaspoon bicarbonate of soda
> 1 level teaspoon cream of tartar
> 25–75g (1–3oz) sugar
> 2 eggs
> 300ml (1/2 pint) sour milk

Mix together all the ingredients into a batter, ideally in a jug. Lightly grease your pan or griddle and heat it. When really hot pour small amounts of the batter on to the surface to form a number of 10-centimetre discs. When nicely browned on the underside, flip them to brown the other side. Eat hot or cold with butter and jam.

Best bacon butties

These are always a winner – just listen to the camp go quiet with satisfaction!

> Fresh white crusty bread
> Butter
> Good local bacon
> Red, brown or yellow sauce

Grill or fry the bacon however you like it (we like it crispy). Slice and butter the bread. Put the bacon in the buttered bread while hot so the butter melts. Argue about which sauce is best. Eat.

Salads, snacks and super-fast things to make

George's Aussie goats' cheese, mango and coriander salad
Mixed green salad leaves
1 big ripe mango, chopped
Lots of fresh coriander leaves
Local goats' cheese
Olive oil; salt and black pepper

Toss together the salad leaves, mango and coriander and crumble the goats' cheese on top. Drizzle some olive oil and season with salt and lots of freshly ground pepper.

Broad bean, pea, runner bean, feta and lemon salad
3 big handfuls podded broad beans
3 big handfuls podded fresh peas
3 big handfuls runner beans
1 block feta cheese
Fresh mint, roughly chopped
Olive oil; juice of 1 lemon

Slice the runner beans and then blanche together with the broad beans and peas for about 4 minutes, until al dente (if you don't want to blanche the peas, keep them separate). Drain and place in a big bowl and allow to cool a little. Crumble in the feta, add the mint and squeeze in the lemon juice and a little olive oil, then mix and eat.

Baked feta and pomegranate salad
1 block feta
1 tablespoon dried oregano
1 tablespoon crushed fennel seeds
Olive oil
2 pomegranates
1 finely chopped cucumber
$\frac{1}{2}$ finely sliced red onion
1 tablespoon honey; 1 clove crushed garlic; juice of 1 lemon;
1 tablespoon chopped mint

Sprinkle the feta with the oregano, fennel seeds and a little olive oil, wrap in foil and bake in the embers of the fire for 5 minutes. Meanwhile put the honey, garlic, lemon juice and chopped mint in a lidded jar or container and shake well to combine. Place the pomegranate seeds, cucumber and onion into a bowl, crumble over the baked feta and pour over the dressing. Pile on to thick slices of toast.

Quick couscous

Couscous is brilliant when camping because you can just add hot water, leave covered for 5 minutes and it's cooked.

Have it as a side dish seasoned well with lemon juice and olive oil. Add lemon and lime zest, fresh grated ginger, caraway seeds, sultanas and a little tamari when you add the water and then add fresh herbs when it's cooked. Add mozzarella, sundried tomatoes, olives and a little pesto. Fry some cooked couscous in a little butter, add a pinch of cinnamon, some sultanas, some freshly chopped parsley, toasted pine nuts and flaked almonds.

Pasta

Pasta can be a lifesaver at camp – if you arrive late or you have some hungry campers, pasta will fill everyone up fast. Try adding cream and spinach to cooked pasta, stir to heat then add some smoked salmon. Or add black-olive pâté or sundried tomato pâté; you could also chuck in olives, ripped-up mozzarella or canned tuna. Add crispy bacon bits, new-season asparagus and fresh parsley.

Noodles

Noodles are another brilliant fast food to eat when you're camping; simply immerse them in boiling water for about 4 to 5 minutes. Add them to miso soup. Make a stir fry with any leftover veggies and fresh herbs, crack over an egg and stir for egg-fried noodles. Make a quick salad by mixing your noodles with a few teaspoons of green curry paste, chopped chilli, a few toasted peanuts, fresh herbs and chopped veggies.

Haloumi cheese

Haloumi (a.k.a. squeaky or loony cheese) is excellent to have when camping. Even though it is sometimes used as a veggie option it's usually the meat eaters who eat it all. You just fry slices in a dry pan or put on skewers to grill over the fire.

Add cooked to salad leaves, fresh herbs and grapes, then drizzle on some olive oil. Season to taste and eat while the cheese is still hot. Make kebabs – cut the haloumi into big cubes and place on skewers alongside bite-size chunks of the vegetables of your choice (cherry tomatoes, button mushrooms, courgettes, peppers and red onions, etc.) And a little pesto, if desired, then grill until deliciously roasted.

Sandwiches

Pork and chargrilled apple sandwiches – core some apples and cut them into whole round slices, then chargrill with thin pork steaks on the campfire. Build your sandwiches with the apple, pork, salad leaves and a squeeze of mustard and mayonnaise.

Cambozola and red-onion marmalade sandwiches

Place cambozola cheese and red-onion marmalade (see page 104) between thick slices of granary bread.

Feta, date and mint sandwiches

Put feta cheese, juicy stoned dates, fresh mint and any lettuce leaves between two slices of bread.

Ollie's strawberry and banana sandwiches

Slice some strawberries and bananas and put between two slices of your favourite bread.

Fisherman's lemons

Mix together 1 tin of dolphin friendly tuna and 2 hard boiled eggs, roughly chopped. Gradually add mayonnaise and lemon juice to your desired consistency. Season to taste and spread into sandwiches or on toast.

Tin-tastic

Squashed-in-the-tin hummus
Open a can of chickpeas and drain the out the water using the lid to stop the chickpeas falling out. Add the juice of a lemon, 3 good lugs of olive oil, some chilli flakes or a chopped fresh chilli, 1 teaspoon of cumin seeds and some chopped wild garlic if you have it. Squash and bash it all together with the implement of your choice and plenty of elbow grease (end of a rolling pin, wooden spoon handle, strong fork, pestle from a pestle and mortar) season with salt and pepper to taste. Spread on some toast, dollop on some fire-baked potatoes or slather some on your salad.

Chick pea, feta, chilli and mint salad
Put 2 cans of chickpeas in a bowl, crumble over a packet of feta cheese, add 1 fresh red chilli (de-seeded and finely chopped) and a handful of roughly chopped mint and flat leaf parsley. Give the salad a generous slug of olive oil, squeeze on some lemon juice, season and mix well.

Black eye beans and sun dried tomatoes
Drain 2 cans of black eyed beans and rinse with some fresh water (you could also use cannellini beans or borlotti beans) empty them into a salad bowl and mix with a packet of rocket and half a jar of sundried tomatoes with a little of their oil. Season and add some shavings of good local hard cheese. Lovely with some crusty bread.

Super-quick snacks

Dad's sausages and marmalade
This snack does sound a bit weird, but it did come from Papa Carr and he loves it. Just barbecue some sausages and serve with marmalade . . . Strange but delicious.

Avocado and tamari
If someone is unhappy at camp this is a sure-fire way to cheer them up. Halve a lovely ripe avocado, remove the stone and pour tamari in the hole. Serve with a teaspoon and wait for the smile.

Grace's oatcakes
Our friend the gorgeous Grace never leaves for a camping trip without a tube of wasabi. Simply spread a little on an oatcake and top with some sliced avocado and sea salt.

Sil's easy-baked camembert fondue

This, along with causing general silly antics at camp is Susila's party trick.

> A round of camembert cheese in its box
> A fat clove garlic, cut into slices
> A little dry white wine (optional)
> Handful fresh herbs, finely chopped (optional)

To serve:
Baguettes, breadsticks, crudités and anything else you like dipping . . .

Take the camembert out of its box, remove all other packaging and place the cheese back in the box. Score some little holes in the top and push in the sliced garlic. Wrap the whole thing in a few layers of tin foil (if you want to add a little wine, pour a very small amount over the top of the cheese while it is half-wrapped). Be creative with your cheese wrapping – try and make it into a sealed, wine tight creation. Place the wrapped cheese in the embers of the campfire for about 10 to 15 minutes. The idea is to allow the cheese to melt to the correct consistency for dipping, so turn it to heat it evenly. Remove from the fire and add a few chopped herbs if you want to. Then simply dig in, fondue-style.

Smoked mackerel pâté with spinach on toast

Once we had discovered this, we found it incredibly hard to stop eating.

Feeds 4:
> 4 fillets smoked mackerel
> Half a jar of horseradish sauce
> Juice of 1 lemon
> Fresh spinach
> Toast

Remove the skin from the mackerel and break up the flesh into a bowl. Add the horseradish and lemon and mash together with a fork. Rinse the spinach and place in a pan with the lid on. Wilt for a minute or so over a moderate heat, season and drizzle over a little olive oil. Spread the pâté on the toast and top with the spinach.

Soups

Soups are souper easy and very warming when you're camping. You can just bung all of your ingredients in a pan and get on with setting up camp or just having fun. Soup has been around way longer than the blender and there is another, far more portable invention that can help get the soup show on the road: the humble potato masher, so don't forget yours.

Red lentil and root vegetable soup with sausages (feeds 4–6)

1 bag (500g) red lentils
Carrots and butternut squash (or whatever root veggies you have), cut into chunks
Fresh herbs (thyme, rosemary and sage are good), chopped
Green vegetables (green beans, broccoli, spinach and peas are good), chopped
Some stock
2 onions, finely chopped
3 cloves garlic, finely chopped
2 leeks, chopped
Good local pork or vegetarian sausages
Olive oil or butter for frying

Over a medium heat, soften the onion and garlic in the olive oil or butter. Add the leeks and fry off a little. Add the carrots and squash and heat through. Add the lentils and enough stock to cover; you may need to add more stock as the lentils cook to maintain a soupy consistency. Add the herbs and simmer for 25 to 30 minutes. Add the green vegetables, 15 minutes before the end of the soup's cooking time. Meanwhile cook the sausages on the fire or stove. Slice into quarters and then when the soup is cooked, season and leave to cool for a few minutes. Eat with the sliced sausages and buttered doorsteps or baked potatoes with heaps of grated cheddar.

Yellow split pea and fennel soup (feeds 4)

1 bag (500g) yellow split peas
3 big bulbs fennel, sliced
Stock
1–2 onions, or 4–5 shallots, chopped
2 cloves garlic, chopped
Milk
Olive oil for frying
A masher

Soften the onions in a little olive oil, add the garlic and sliced fennel and cook until the edges start to brown. Add the bag of split peas and cover with stock. Put the lid on the pan and simmer for 30 minutes, adding more stock if needed. When the split peas are soft with a slight bite remove from the heat, add a little milk and mash. Season with salt and lots of black pepper; add a few crushed fennel seeds if you have them.

Tess's 10-minute miso soup

This is fantastic when camping; it's very quick to make, nutritious and tasty. Miso contains living enzymes that aid digestion and strengthen the blood and it's stuffed full of B vitamins. Fresh miso is available at all good health-food shops.

Makes a big pot, feeds 6–8:
  4–5 pints water
  4 cloves garlic, roughly chopped
  1 good-sized nobble of ginger, roughly chopped
  1 red chilli, deseeded and roughly chopped
  2 good lugs tamari
  3 heaped tablespoons fresh barley miso
  Toasted sesame oil
  2 limes

Enough chopped vegetables for whoever is eating – you can use broccoli, purple sprouting broccoli, carrots, spring onions, radish, mangetout, sugarsnap peas, spinach, chard, watercress, sprouted seeds.

Put the water in a big saucepan. Add the ginger, garlic, chilli and tamari and bring to simmering point but don't boil. Add the miso, keeping the pan on the heat but taking care that the soup doesn't boil (miso's enzymes are destroyed at boiling point). Add the chopped vegetables, cook for just a minute and remove from the heat. The vegetables don't need to be cooked – the idea is to warm them up and keep them as fresh as possible, preserving their goodness. Serve in big bowls with some soba noodles or steamed rice on the side and drizzle with a little oil and lime juice if desired. For something extra special top with some pan-fried tuna with a sesame crust.

Aaron's pan-fried tuna or salmon with a sesame crust

This is perfect to go on the miso soup but you can also have it sliced on a salad or with baked potatoes. You can use any good fillet of fish but tuna and salmon taste best with the miso soup.

  Fresh tuna steak or salmon fillet
  Black and white sesame seeds
  Groundnut or sesame oil

Put a generous amount of sesame seeds onto a board or plate. Press the fillet into the seeds on both sides making sure it is completely covered. Heat a lug of oil in a frying pan. Add the tuna to the pan when the oil is hot. Sear for about 2 minutes on each side depending how thick it is and how rare you like it. Serve on top of the miso soup.

One-pot wonders

Sam's chicken dinner

This is great for a few reasons: you can put the dinner on then go and have fun; it's really juicy; it's easy to make and feeds loads of people; and you can make soup from it the next day – two meals in one.

    1 big massive pot
    1 medium-size happy free-range organic chicken
    1 onion, thinly sliced
    2 leeks, thinly sliced
    8 carrots, cut in half widthways then in half lengthways
    Tamari or soy sauce, or worcester sauce, or 1 teaspoon of marmite or honey,
        or any combination of these
    3 stock cubes
    Baby new potatoes
    A splash of white or red wine (optional)
    A few fresh or dried herbs, chopped

Put the chicken in the pot, along with all the other ingredients except the potatoes and carrots. Fill with enough water to cover the chicken, crumble over the stock cubes and bring to the boil. Reduce the heat, put the lid on and simmer for about 1 hour.

After 1 hour, skim off any scum that you see floating on the surface of the stew. Add the potatoes, cook for a further 10 minutes then add the carrots. When the potatoes are cooked remove the pan from the heat, take out the chicken and discard its skin. Carve the chicken and put a serving in each bowl, together with vegetables and finally a couple or ladlefuls of broth. Serve with a chunk of bread on the side to soak up all the good bits at the bottom of your bowl.

. . . Sam's tasty tasty leftover chicken soup

This recipe uses the leftovers from the above chicken dinner. Pick out any remaining meat from the pot and set aside. Return the carcass to the pot along with any leftover veggies. Add some water and bring to the boil. Turn the heat down and allow to simmer for an hour or two. Strain and serve in bowls with the torn-up chicken and some crusty bread. You can add some noodles or macaroni if you fancy.

Risottos

You might not think that risottos are very practical when camping because you have to keep stirring, but it's actually one of the nicest and easiest things to cook at camp. Sitting over just one pot, with a glass or two of vino while you have a good old chinwag is not much effort at all. We like to get everyone to have a stir for Christmas-pudding good luck.

Basic risotto
Feeds 6–8 hungry campers
    500g carnaroli or arborio rice
    1½ large glasses dry white wine
    2 pints of stock
    Big chunk of parmesan cheese
    Butter
    2 shallots or 1 onion, finely chopped
    2 cloves garlic, finely chopped
    Salt and black pepper

In a large, heavy-based saucepan melt the butter and add the shallots or onions. Cook over a gentle heat until translucent, then add the garlic and cook for 1–2 minutes. Add the rice and stir for 5 minutes, until every grain of rice is glistening with butter. Turn up the heat and add a big glass of wine. Keep stirring. When the rice has soaked up the wine add the remaining wine. Keep stirring. When the rice has soaked this up add a cup of stock. Keep stirring. Repeat the process, adding a cup of stock when the rice has absorbed the liquid, until the rice is al dente (usually about 18–20 minutes), stirring continuously. When the rice is cooked remove from the heat, stir in a knob of butter and some grated parmesan. Season to taste and serve with a massive salad.

The above recipe is delicious as it is but you can add whatever you fancy towards the end of cooking. Some other risotto combinations are:
- Asparagus, pea and lemon
- Ricotta, leek and butternut squash
- Chicken, bacon, parmesan and peas (naughty but very nice)
- Prawn and asparagus or samphire
- Lemon, rocket and pancetta
- Wild mushroom
- Artichoke heart and pecorino
- Butternut squash, feta and thyme

Pasta and Casseroles

Kat and Fred's red sauce

A simple red sauce taught to us by a genuine Italian mama's boy is often the basis of many a camping feast.

Gently heat a good lug of olive oil in a pan and add 3 finely chopped cloves of garlic. Stir for two minutes ensuring that the garlic just heats through without colouring. Add a tin of chopped plum tomatoes, a teaspoon of sugar and plenty of salt and pepper. Simmer for 25 minutes, with the lid off, stirring occasionally. Serve with spaghetti and a grating of parmesan cheese.

Camping meatballs like mama used to make

Some good quality 100% beef burgers – 2 per person
Smoked bacon or some tasty olives or both!
Ingredients for a red sauce
Spaghetti – fresh is quicker
Parmesan and basil to serve

Break each burger into four to six pieces and roll into small balls. Take a small strip of bacon and push into the centre of each meatball, do the same with the olives. Heat up a good lug of oil in a large pan. When it's hot add the meatballs – they should pop and spit a bit. Occasionally turn the meatballs and, when browned all over, transfer them to a plate. Discard the oil, return the pan to the stove or fire and reduce the heat. Make the red sauce as normal, adding the meatballs five minutes after you've added the tomatoes.

Sausage casserole (serves 4–6)

2 packs good quality sausages or chipolatas
5 shallots, quartered (halved if they're small)
Smoked lardons or good quality smoked bacon, chopped
Ingredients for a red sauce

Fry the sausages until golden all over, add the shallots and lardons and cook for a few more minutes until the shallots are coloured and the lardons are crispy. Now simply make the red sauce in the pan with the other ingredients. Serve with fire baked potatoes or crusty bread.

. . . other ideas for your red sauce:
- Stir in some crème fraîche for a creamy sauce.
- Add some prawns, two dollops of Greek yoghurt and chopped flat-leaf parsley
- Fry some chilli with the garlic and add some clams in their shells 10 minutes before the end.

The sauce is ready when the shells are open.

Feasts

Cooking up a big evening feast is one of the highlights of our camping day. You've spent the day racing around outside and it's finally time to reward yourself for all that hard work. It's just magical when everyone pulls together and gets involved in the creation of an amazing array of delicious dishes. These are a few of our favourite feast ideas and we hope you enjoy making and eating them as much as we do.

Fish

Fish is one of the simplest things to cook when you're camping; you can just pop it on the campfire with nothing more complicated than a squeeze of lemon and a drizzle of olive oil and it's guaranteed to knock your socks off. When you're camping near the sea it's even better because you can try out the local catches, experiment with different herbs and spices and even go fishing yourself. We both adore fish, as do most of our camping circle (except Dylan), and it is usually the only food that everybody is happy to eat.

When you are buying fish:
- Find out how fresh it is; ask when it was caught.
- Ask where it was caught.
- Choose fish with clear, shiny, sparkling eyes.
- A firm fish is a good fish.

How to clean a fish

You'll need:

A very sharp knife

A spoon

Some newspaper

As soon as possible after buying or catching your fish, wash it in cold running water. This removes the fish's protective slime and makes it easier to handle. If you need to de-scale it, do so now. Not all fish needs de-scaling; if the scales are large and flat, they should be removed. Lay the fish flat and, using the dull edge of the knife at almost a 90-degree angle, scrape along the fish in short strokes moving from the tail to the head. Remember that this is can be a very messy job and the scales can fly everywhere, so do it with your hands and the fish inside a carrier bag. When the fish is smooth and scale-free wash it again under running water.

To clean your fish, place it on some newspaper and cut from the gills along the belly to the vent (the small anal opening near the tail). Open up the fish and remove the innards, throat and gills with your hands. The innards and throat should pull away easily but it's often necessary to cut the gills away with a knife. Do take care, as the little fishy insides are fragile and you don't want the contents of the guts going everywhere. Nearly done now – scrape along the backbone inside the body cavity using your spoon to remove the blood vein. Wash the fish thoroughly once again in cold water.

Remember . . .

- Use plenty of newspaper – it soaks up the blood and once you've cleaned the fish you can simply wrap up and dispose of the innards.
- Always cut away from you so that you are less likely to cut yourself if your hands slip.
- It's true what they say – a sharp knife is a safe knife.
- The less you struggle the safer you will be.

The fish grill

A fish grill is two wire grills hinged together. You simply place the fish between the grills, close and adjust until the fish is secured. They are widely available and you can get all different sizes. They are great for cooking stuffed fish over the fire or barbecue as they hold everything in place and you can cook quite a few fish at once in the bigger ones.

Simply grilled fish

Grilling is the easiest way to cook your fish. Choose smaller fish, which will cook right through before they have a chance to burn. Any fish are great – mackerel, sardine, bass, trout, salmon – anything you fancy that's looking good.

Simply squeeze on some lemon juice and season well. Grill whole on the barbecue or over the fire until cooked to perfection. Squeeze over more lemon juice and eat.

You can make posh sardines on toast – grill some sardines and when cooked remove the heads and tails. Using a fork, mash together with some lemon zest and parsley. Serve on toast with a squeeze of lemon juice . . . How simple is that!

Or serve your grilled fish with lots of fresh-lemon wedges, chips from the local chip shop and a view of the sea.

Fennel-stuffed trout with fresh herbs

You can also use sea bass, gurnard, bream and salmon for this recipe.

1 whole trout, de-scaled and gutted
1 fennel bulb, thinly sliced
Fresh herbs, chopped
1 lemon, sliced
Olive oil
Salt and black pepper

Rub the outside of the fish with a little olive oil and seasoning. Stuff the fish with the fennel and herbs (use the fennel tops too), lemon slices and a drizzle of oil. Close the fish and place it in the fish grill. Grill for about 5 minutes each side or until cooked through, depending on the size of the fish and the heat of the fire. Serve with lots of freshly squeezed lemon juice.

Baked fish in the Sunday newspapers

This is a good way to use your campfire for cooking lots of fish for lots of people and recycle the Sunday papers at the same time. The size of the fish doesn't matter; big fish take longer to cook, of course, but look very impressive (large salmon and sea bass are brilliant cooked in this way).

Dip a sheet of newspaper in water and quickly wrap it around the fish. Repeat until you've got about 10 sheets around each fish, then tie up with string. Place the parcel or parcels in the embers and turn occasionally. (You might think the paper would catch fire but that's why the water's there. Do have some more water handy, though, in case the paper does ignite and you need to dampen it again.) The guideline when cooking in an oven is 15 minutes per kilo, but heat in a fire can be more intense so you should adjust the time accordingly – you can always shove the fish back in if it's not ready. Basically it's time to check when the newspaper really starts to blacken. Open your parcel and push a knife into the densest part of the fish, near the backbone: a little resistance means your fish is cooked; too much resistance means it needs a little longer.

Whole baked salmon in the fire

    1 whole salmon (de-scaled and gutted)
    The weekend papers
    String
    2 lemons (1 sliced)
    1 lime, sliced
    Olive oil
    2 big handfuls mixed fresh herbs, chopped – for example, basil, lemon thyme,
        parsley, tarragon, wild garlic, wild thyme

Stuff the fish with the lemon and lime slices and as many herbs as possible. Wrap in newspaper, following the instructions above. Cook in the fire for 20–25 minutes or until the paper blackens (it really depends on the size of the fish and the heat of the fire), then check to see if your fish is cooked; return to the fire if necessary. When cooked, remove from the paper and serve with freshly squeezed lemon juice. Wait for the squeals of joy.

Simple foil-baked fish

This method is great for whole fish as well as fillets and steaks. For whole fish: stuff with whatever you like then wrap in a couple of layers of tin foil and bake in the hot embers until cooked through. For fillets and steaks: marinate in whatever you fancy (or just slather your fish with marinade/pesto/tamari, etc.) Then wrap in a couple of layers of tin foil and bake in the fire until cooked through.

Amelia's coconut marinade

You can use any firm fish for this. You can marinate the fish before you leave or while you're setting up camp.

The zest and juice of 1 lime
2 cloves of garlic finely chopped
2 tablespoons of finely sliced fresh ginger
1 red chilli de-seeded and thinly sliced
A handful of dried or desiccated coconut
4 tablespoons of coconut milk
A handful ripped up fresh coriander
2 lemon grass stalks with hard outer leaves removed and chopped finely
Some sesame oil (olive oil or chilli oil are just as good)

Amelia's ginger teriyaki marinade – this is especially good on salmon

Half a bottle of teriyaki sauce – use more to tantalise your taste buds!
The juice and some of the zest of 1 lime
The juice of 1 lemon
A good handful of ripped up coriander leaves
2–3 cloves of garlic – crushed and cut up very roughly
A good grating of ginger root, about 1 inch square of ginger
Some black pepper, but no salt as the fish and the teriyaki sauce are salty enough
A tablespoon of sesame oil – helps it to cook and adds a slightly nutty taste

For both the marinades mix the ingredients together in the container and marinate the fish for about an hour. Then lay the fish onto a piece of foil make a pocket so there is still an air pocket inside the foil. Make sure there are no holes. Simply place on a grill over the fire or in the campfire itself. Shake the packet with tongs every once in a while to make sure the fish is getting coated with lovely marinade juices. Cooking time is very quick, about 10 minutes – longer if the fire is cooler. If you fancy, heat up the remaining marinade in a small pan and spoon it over the fish once cooked.

Enjoy,
love Amelia x

Poached fish

This is a very gentle way to cook fish that lets the subtlety of the flavours gently float out. You can poach in water but we like to poach in milk for a really creamy taste. The used milk is also great for pouring on to your hot baked potatoes. Firmer fish are better for poaching – haddock, cod, halibut and salmon are ideal – and it needs to be filleted.

Poached un-dyed smoked haddock

The Carrs were brought up on this easy-peasy and exceedingly yummy dish. You can cook it in a fire or on a stove in a pan.

$\frac{1}{2}$ fish fillet per person
Milk
Butter
Black pepper

If cooking on the fire, place each fillet on a separate piece of tin foil. Then pull up the sides and wrap around the fish to make a basin. Pour in enough milk to cover the fillet. Add a knob of butter and some black pepper. Close up the foil to make a parcel then wrap in another piece of foil. Place on the grill and bake over the fire for about 10 minutes. Be careful with the parcels – foil tears easily and you don't want to lose any of the milk.

If you're cooking on the stove, place the fillets in a saucepan and cover with milk. Add a knob of butter and some pepper. Heat gently, taking care not to boil the milk, until the flesh is cooked through and becomes opaque.

Pan-fried fish

You can pan-fry nearly any fish, whole (if you've a big enough pan) or filleted, so if you haven't got a fire and are cooking on a stove this is super-fast way of cooking up a fish treat.

Pan-fried sole
1 sole fillet per person
Butter
A little seasoned flour
1 lemon

Melt a knob of butter in a pan, dust the fillets in the seasoned flour and fry for about 5 minutes each side. Serve with a generous squeeze of lemon juice and chips.

Meat

Fred's favourite fillet-steak sandwich

This is a camping classic that tastes even better after you've hunted and gathered your dinner at the local butcher's or farm shop and cooked it out in the open air. Truly a taste sensation.

> Enough fillet steak (or sirloin or rump) for everyone
> Enough of your favourite crusty baps for everyone
> Rocket or other peppery leaves
> 2 red onions thinly sliced
> Few vine-ripened tomatoes, sliced
> Wholegrain mustard
> Cheese (optional)
> Butter for frying

Place the onions in a pan with some butter and cook over a gentle heat until sticky and translucent. Turn up the heat (or move to a hotter part of the fire) and stir, letting the edges brown and caramelise. Meanwhile smother the steaks in some wholegrain mustard and cook on a grill for 5–6 minutes on each side for medium (for rare, 2–3 minutes each side; for well done, 10 minutes each side). Remove from the heat and leave to rest for a couple of minutes.

Slice open the baps and add the onions, then the tomato, rocket and cheese, if using. Divide the steak between the baps, give them a little squeeze and devour.

Kat's stroganoff

Kat's winning camping dinner.

Feeds 6:
> 1 onion, finely chopped
> About 20 button mushrooms, halved
> 2 fillets good-quality beef, cut into strips
> 1 big tablespoon wholegrain or dijon mustard
> 1 large pot crème fraîche
> Olive oil for frying

Heat some oil in a pan, add the onions and cook till softened. Add the mushrooms and fry until browned. Smother the strips of beef in mustard and add to the pan. Fry until the meat is sealed, turn down the heat and add the crème fraîche, stir and heat through gently for a couple of minutes, don't allow to boil or the mixture will separate. Serve with rice and lots of steaming greens.

**SWEET APPLE
FARM**

CAMPING
AND
CARAVANING
AVAILABLE

►

A nice piece of pork from Sam and Jane

1 pork loin strip
At least 12 rashers of smoked streaky bacon
Soy sauce or tamari
Runny honey

Lay the strips of bacon in a row along a chopping board and place your pork loin in the middle. Wrap the bacon around the pork from both sides, keeping a consistent pattern with the ends of the bacon meeting down the middle of the pork. Then carefully turn the pork over, so that all the bacon 'knots' are on the underside. Mix together a little soy sauce (or tamari) and honey, then brush the topside with the mixture. Slowly barbecue the pork, for about 15 minutes on each side, cooking the underside first to seal together the bacon joins. When the meat's cooked, remove from the heat, slice from one end and serve.

This is particularly nice with Sam's barbecue sauce; which in short is:

A bottle tomato ketchup
A large tablespoon honey
A large teaspoon wholegrain mustard
A good dollop tamari or soy sauce
A dollop of Worcestershire sauce
A lug red wine
A pinch cajun spices
A lug of extra virgin olive oil
Mix and dip

Tess and Karn's camping curry special

This is camping comfort food and is great when you have lots of people to feed. Pre-cooking the butternut squash or pumpkin makes the curry even creamier. Have an Indian feast at camp and try cooking chapatis on a spade.

The spices:
>1 teaspoon black mustard seeds
>3 teaspoons turmeric
>1 tablespoon crushed cumin seeds
>1 tablespoon crushed coriander seeds
>1 tablespoon crushed fennel seeds

Crush and mix together before you leave home and store in a sealed container.

>1 big butternut squash or pumpkin, peeled, de-seeded and roughly chopped
>2 cans chickpeas
>5 big handfuls spinach
>Enough lamb or chicken for everyone, cubed (optional)
>1 cauliflower, chopped
>2 big onions, finely chopped
>1 fennel bulb, finely sliced
>2 cloves garlic, finely chopped
>1 red chilli, finely chopped
>1 cube ginger, finely chopped
>1 pack creamed coconut
>Vegetable stock
>Ground nut oil
>Fresh coriander, roughly chopped

Boil or steam the squash or pumpkin for about 10 minutes in a pan. Drain, saving the water if possible, and set aside. Heat some oil in a pan and sweat off the onions for a couple of minutes, then add the ginger and chilli and cook for a few more minutes. Add the garlic and spices and gently fry for a few minutes, until they release their aroma and start popping. Add the fennel and the meat (if using) and brown for a couple of minutes. Add the cauliflower and stir to coat with spices. Add the chickpeas, creamed coconut and a little stock made with some of the squash water. Simmer gently for about 30 minutes. Add the squash and spinach and simmer for a further 5 minutes. Remove from the heat, stir in some fresh coriander and serve. This is fantastic eaten the next day when the flavours have developed even more.

Raita

Lemon raita: grate the zest of a lemon into a big pot of plain yoghurt and add a little lemon juice.

Cucumber and coriander raita: finely chop some cucumber and tear up a few coriander leaves, add to a big pot of plain or Greek yoghurt.

Chapatis on a spade
If you don't have a fire, you can hold each chapati over the flame on your
camping stove.

> 2 cups wholemeal or plain flour
> Pinch of salt
> Water as needed

Mix together the flour and salt and add enough water to make a soft dough. Knead
until soft and pliable, then break off walnut-sized pieces and roll into round balls. Dust
with a little flour and roll or press out into flat discs. Heat the blade end of the spade
over the fire. One at a time, place the discs on the hot spade and cook in the fire; when
the edges start browning, turn the chapati over and cook the other side.

Rice-paper roll-ups

These summery rolls are flippin' brilliant to eat when you're camping – they're no-cook DIY food, great for lots of people. Don't be put off by the huge list of ingredients; you won't use them all, just whatever you fancy. The only essential ingredient is the rice-papers, which are thin discs, also used for spring rolls. You'll find them in chinese food shops and some big supermarkets. They come in two sizes; the larger ones are better because you can stuff more in them.

You'll need:
    1 packet rice papers
    1 or 2 bowls hot water

Choose a selection of the following fillings:
    Avocado, sliced (essential)
    Carrot, julienned
    Cucumber, julienned
    Wilted spinach with lemon juice
    Watercress
    Mint, roughly chopped
    Rocket, roughly chopped
    Flat-leaf parsley, roughly chopped
    Tofu – smoked/with basil/fried, thinly sliced
    Nori seaweed sheets, torn
    Crab sticks
    Spring onions, sliced lengthways
    Buttery garlic prawns
    Super-thin rice noodles, cooked
    Edamame (soy beans)
    Campfire-baked fish

. . . and some of these for dipping:
    Sweet chilli sauce
    Plum sauce
    Tamari or soy sauce
    Sesame seeds
    Mayonnaise

Put your chosen fillings in piles on a large tray or plate. Get the hot water ready (not too hot or it will burn fingers), grab a rice paper each and take it in turns to submerge your papers in the bowl of hot water. Soak them for a couple of minutes, until soft, shake off the excess water, and lay out flat on a plate. Layer your fillings in a line towards one side of your paper. Fold the nearest edge over the filling and hold in place with one finger. Fold in the sides to make an envelope shape and roll the whole thing away from you (it sounds complicated but when you have one in front of you it will all make sense).

Dip the rolls in the sauce of your choice. Eat, repeat, eat, repeat, eat, repeat . . .

Vegetables

There's no reason why you can't enjoy lovely fresh vegetables when you're camping – just keep them in a cool place until ready to use. You can't beat fire-roasted veggies or fresh greens picked the same day and eaten with your fire-baked fish.

Greens with olive oil, lemon juice and sea salt

A big bowl of fresh, steaming vegetables served with fish or meat from your campfire tastes amazing. It's so simple we can't rave about it enough. Fresh greens are really easy to find when you're away camping, and so easy to prepare. Just wash them, put them in the saucepan with a little water, blanche for 2–3 minutes, strain, drizzle on some olive oil, squeeze on some lemon juice and season. Fantastic.

Great greens are spinach, broccoli, kale, beans, peas, broad beans, purple sprouting broccoli, chard, asparagus, spring greens, cabbage and samphire (see page 224 for when they're in season).

Baked peppers with goats' cheese

Romano, red, yellow or orange peppers,
Soft goats' cheese
Fresh herbs, roughly chopped

Cut out the stem and scoop out the seeds of each pepper, leaving the peppers whole. Stuff with the goats' cheese and herbs and wrap in foil. Alternatively, halve and de-seed the peppers, stuff each half with the goats' cheese and herbs, put the two halves back together and wrap tightly in foil. Put the wrapped peppers in the embers of the fire or on the grill to roast for about 8 minutes, turning occasionally.

Chargrilled butternut squash or pumpkin with wild thyme

1 butternut squash and/or pumpkin, sliced and washed but not peeled,
Olive oil
Wild thyme or rosemary, roughly chopped

Drizzle a little olive oil over the squash or pumpkin and sprinkle with the herbs. Chargrill the slices on the grill over the fire or on a barbecue.

Bacon and vegetables

Bacon goes beautifully with many vegetables; it must be the natural seasoning from the sweet salty flavour that heightens the taste of earthy goodness. Choose only one vegetable and enjoy the simplicity of the combination. Good vegetables you can try are sliced cabbage, shredded brussels sprouts, sticks of carrot, parsnip peelings or wedges of fresh beetroot.

Just fry chopped bacon until crispy and sizzling. Add the vegetable of your choice and cook until golden and meltingly tender. Finish off with a good helping of freshly ground black pepper. If you need your carbohydrates, then chuck in some cooked pasta.

Baked potatoes

Baked potatoes are traditional camping fare and taste amazing cooked in a campfire. Just wash your potatoes, prod them a few times with a fork, rub a little olive oil over each one and sprinkle with a little salt. Wrap in foil and place in the fire, turning at intervals (using tongs!) until cooked. Serve with butter or olive oil and pepper or with squashed hummus, pesto or cheese.

New potatoes with peas and crushed fennel seeds

Boil some new-season new potatoes and some fresh peas. Strain and serve with a little butter and some crushed fennel seeds.

Sweet potatoes

Baked sweet potatoes are also brilliant; they're just as delicious as potatoes and quicker to cook. Simply wash and wrap in foil twice (don't prod or all the juices come out) then put in the embers of the campfire until baked. Slice down the middle, add a big spoonful of soft cheese or chilli butter and eat with fresh grilled fish and some steaming greens.

Baked beetroot with crème fraîche and chives

Beetroot are delicious baked in the fire; they take a little longer to cook than potatoes but are worth the wait, so choose small, firm beets. Scrub the beetroot, taking care not to break the skins. Place in some tin foil and make a loose parcel so the beets steam a little as well as bake. Put in the embers of fire for about 1 hour, depending on the size of beetroot and the heat of the fire.

Fire-baked whole vegetables

You can fire-bake whole squash, onions, carrots and leeks. To bake squash, just cut in half (OK, so it's not actually whole), remove the seeds and bake in foil; bake whole onions in their skins in foil; bake carrots and leeks whole in foil. Remember to keep turning the parcels so they cook evenly.

Corn on the cob

Another winning camping food and so easy to prepare – though you do have to decide how much charring you like on your corn. Wrap in foil if you don't like any. Otherwise, dampen the husks and remove the grassy inner lining for a slight char. For lots of char remove the husk altogether, soak in water for 10 minutes and then cook, turning often. Now for the best bit: dress with lots of butter, freshly milled pepper and sea salt.

Tomatoes

Wrap a few tomatoes together in foil with a splash of olive oil, some black olives and chunks of mozzarella. When cooked, add torn basil leaves. Or cut some tomatoes in half, toss with a tin of cannellini beans, olive oil, crushed fennel and cumin seeds, crushed garlic and chopped chilli. Wrap in foil and bake in the fire for 10–15 minutes. Serve with fresh coriander.

'Truly great friends are hard to find, difficult
to leave and impossible to forget.'
G. Randolf

Puddings

Puddings and chocolate are a very important part of life, camping and otherwise. They are essential as they have magical properties, including being able to stop tears midflow, providing instant pain relief, giving super-human energy and special flirting powers. We believe you should never go camping without chocolate as you never know when you might need it.

Juliette's so-simple chocolate mousse

This is great to make when you're camping as it's not necessary to refrigerate it and if you use soya cream you can buy it before you go and it doesn't go off.

300ml carton of thick double cream or soya cream
2 x 150g bars of 70% dark chocolate (basically equal parts chocolate to cream)

Melt the chocolate in a bowl over simmering water. Remove from the heat and leave to cool slightly. Mix in the cream and leave to set in a cool place. Try using a scented chocolate for a different flavour, or add some brandy for a kick or some chilli for an even bigger kick.

Stuff dipped in chocolate

As you've probably guessed, we love chocolate. Hence why we love dipping things in it.

Some good things to dip: almonds, brazil nuts, walnuts, fingers, dried mango, strawberries, cherries, bananas, dates.

Melt two 100g bars of good quality dark chocolate in bowl over some simmering water – resist the temptation to stir. Dip in your treats and eat warm or leave to set in a cool, shaded place.

Classic baked banana with chocolate and pecans

Fruit is fantastic to make puddings with at camp – and, handily, it goes amazingly well with chocolate. If you're lucky enough to have a campfire you can bake many fruits really easily

1 banana per person
150g bar of dark chocolate (minimum 70% cocoa solids)
Some chopped pecans

Using a sharp knife, cut lengthways through the skin of each banana to make a slit. Squash in some pieces of chocolate and a few nuts and push the slit back together. Wrap in foil and place in the white embers of the fire or on the grill of your barbecue for about 5 minutes. Unwrap carefully and eat with a spoon.

Other ways to snazzy up your baked bananas:

- Add some brandy and chopped almonds and serve with cinnamon-dusted cream
- Pour in some runny honey with bashed pistachio nuts. Serve with fresh cream.
- Place whole, unpeeled bananas on the grill for 10 minutes, turning as the skin blackens, then split open and serve with brandy cream.

Fire-baked peaches

Cut a few peaches in half and remove the stones. Stuff each peach half with ricotta flavoured with a little almond essence or amaretto and a few flaked or chopped almonds. Put the halves back together and wrap in foil, leaving a small hole at the top. Pour in some runny honey and sprinkle with few more almonds. Close up the hole and bake in the hot coals – make sure the hole is upright. Serve with cream if you fancy.

Blackberry marscapone camping pudding

Per person you will need:

 100g/4oz mascarpone cheese
 1 tablespoon ground almonds
 1 teaspoon of your favourite liquor – Cointreau, Tia Maria, amaretto
  and brandy work well
 25g/1oz caster sugar
 Freshly picked soft fruit – blackberries and raspberries work very well

Beat the mascarpone in a bowl with a wooden spoon until it starts to soften, then add the sugar and continue to beat till creamy. Gradually stir in the ground almonds and liquor. Cover with fruit and serve.

Tess's camping tiramisu

This is such a super-simple yet very impressive pudding – brilliant for showing off.

 Couple of packets of ginger nut biscuits (cheap ones are better)
 Some sherry (you could use brandy but it would be very alcoholic)
 Couple of big cartons of whipping or double cream

Whisk the cream in a big bowl till it forms nice peaks (you can delegate this task to some nice chap or chapess with big biceps). Put some sherry in a small bowl and one by one dip the biscuits in the sherry for about 4 seconds – don't leave them in too long or they'll go soggy. Using a teaspoonful of cream, stick 2 dipped biscuits together and put them on their sides on a plate. With another teaspoonful of cream, stick another dipped biscuit on to the two on the plate; repeat until you've got something resembling a ginger-nut caterpillar on the plate. Make 2 or 3 such caterpillars side by side on the plate. Cover with the rest of the cream for a cream-covered surprise. If you're making this as a birthday cake, decorate with candles or some bashed-up organic chocolate. Leave somewhere shaded for a little while, until everything's melted together, then serve with a big, smug smile.

Drinks

Sunset chai

This drink was inspired by a trip to India and the spice markets of Fort Cochin. It's so quick to make. Just store in an airtight jam jar until ready to use.

Mix together equal amounts of cardamom pods, broken cinnamon sticks and cloves, grate some fresh nutmeg into the mixture. Put it all in the jar and shake it to mix.

When you fancy a cup of sunset chai you need:

    Your sunset chai mix

    Rice milk, soya milk or cow's milk – 1 cup of milk per person

    Local honey

    Brandy (optional)

Put the milk in a saucepan and add one tablespoon of spice mix and one teaspoon of honey per person. Heat the milk gently being careful not to boil, when hot pour into cups and add a capful of brandy to each cup. A perfect accompaniment to any sunset!

Brandy coffee

Brandy coffee is another of our camping traditions. It's especially good at festivals and is a great way to start the day. Having a cup of fresh coffee outside your tent in the morning feels so decadent, so taking a coffee maker is vital. Italian percolators are ideal for camping and they make camp smell lovely.

To make brandy coffee: simply brew a fresh pot of coffee; meanwhile pour a capful of brandy into each person's cup and then add the coffee and a spoon of honey and milk as you wish.

Cherry or raspberry cava

There is always something to celebrate – whether it's an engagement, a birthday or whose got the best tan line – and this is the perfect drink to do it with.

>   Good cava or champagne
>   Fresh cherries or raspberries
>   Cherry brandy or raspberry cassis

Pour a little cherry brandy or raspberry cassis into each glass (ideally you should use champagne flutes, but any will do). Add a couple of cherries or raspberries and top up cava or champagne.

CAMPING PEANUT BRITTLE
1 bag caster sugar (organic if you can get it)
1 bag roasted, salted peanuts (pistachios, almonds and cashews also
work well)

Cover a heatproof flat surface, such as a bread board or tree
stump, with tin foil. Open the bag of nuts then hold it closed
while you bash them with a rolling pin or something else heavy.
Slowly melt the sugar in a heavy-based saucepan over a medium heat
without stirring. When all the sugar has dissolved, allow to deepen
in colour slightly but be careful not to burn it. Remove from the
heat and carefully pour on to the prepared surface to make a flat,
misshapen blob.
Immediately sprinkle the nuts on the sugar liquid and leave to set.
When the brittle is fully cooled, break it into random shards. They
can be eaten straight away or stored for later when you need some
energy.

Fun stuff to make

Here are some fun recipes to try, all of which are great if you have kids or are a big kid yourself. Don't forget about good old toasted marshmallows.

Campfire biscuits

Just imagine: dawn is breaking, a feathery mist is kissing the valley below, the smell of coffee is wafting through the morning dew and someone has handed you a hot, crumbly morsel melting with butter and jam . . . perfect.

You'll need a stick, approximately 1cm (½in) thick and between 50cm and 1m (2–4ft) long. Try substituting some of the flour for rolled porridge oats and adding some mixed spice.

85g (3oz or 6 level tablespoons) butter
55g (2oz or 4 level tablespoons) soft brown sugar
2 cups plain flour
2 eggs

Beat together the butter and sugar, add the flour and eggs and mix well to make the biscuit dough. Wrap the end of your stick with foil. Make a ball of dough roughly the size of a small tangerine and push this on to the end of the stick – not all the way through but enough for it to be secure. Hold the stick over the hot coals of your fire until the biscuit is a rich, golden brown on the outside. Pull the biscuit off the stick and fill the hole that's left with rich organic butter and preferably homemade jam.

Campfire popcorn

You'll need a stick long enough to hold at arm's length to your fire. Place 1 teaspoon of oil and 1 tablespoon of popcorn kernels in the centre of a large piece of foil. Bring together the corners of the foil, sealing them firmly to make a pocket and remembering to leave enough room for the corn to pop. Make a loop with your excess foil to wrap round the stick. Hold the parcel over the hot coals, shaking constantly until the corn stops popping. Serve with a generous sprinkling of salt or some melted butter and honey.

bird kite

1   Photocopy or trace the bird and cut out the shape.
2   Fold it in half with the black side inside.
3   Staple three times down the body near to the fold. When you staple the tail end, attach approximately three metres of streamer tail (you can use lightweight ribbon or cut-up plastic bags).
4   Punch a hole as indicated.
5   Spread out the wings, black side up, and staple straw as indicated. The straw should reach the wing tips. You can attach two straws together if your straw isn't long enough.
6   Attach string (use light cotton or fishing line) by passing one end down through one hole, passing it round the back and up through the other hole, then tie tightly in a knot.
7   Tie the loose end of the line round a strong stick, wrapping up any excess.

This little bird kite is very quick and easy to make. It doesn't fly to great heights but flutters and follows you around like a pet on a string. Here are some tips to get it airborne:

- Hold up your bird with the black side towards the wind and let the line out; if there is enough wind your bird will fly straight up. Let it fly away from you then pull gently on the line to get some more height, repeat this until your bird is as high as you can get it.
- If the bird sinks tail-first there might not be enough wind. Ask a friend to hold the kite up, away from you with their back to the wind. When they release the kite gradually pull hand over hand on the line to gain height.
- If it dives head-first or spins there might be too much wind. The tail adds stability in strong winds so try adding some more. You can also try moving the hole where the string is attached; nearer the head in higher winds and towards the tail in lower winds.

Good games

Kick the bucket

We used to play this for hours and hours when we were kids and it is still a winner. It's best to play where there are lots of hiding places – woods are perfect. You need a bucket or something that makes a noise when you kick it.

Someone is elected 'on' and must guard the bucket while everyone else goes to hide. The guard must look away and loudly count to fifty, after which they must go in search of the hiding players. The aim of the game is to kick the bucket before the seeker sees you and kicks the bucket himself. If the seeker sees you and kicks the bucket before you do, you are out of the game.

Sports day

Why not organise a sports day? You won't need many props and they cause much hilarity – it's a great way to get to know everyone on your campsite. Possible events are: an egg-and-spoon race, a sleeping-bag sack race (only on dry days), a wheelbarrow race and a three-legged race (four-legged if you're daring); and synchronised swimming minus the water will get you laughing all the way to the winner's podium – an upturned box, of course.

British bulldog

This is an old favourite; you'll need a field or large space on the beach. Draw or make two parallel lines on the ground, about fifty metres apart. One person is the catcher and stands in between the two lines. Everyone else stands in a row on one line – they are the bulldogs. The bulldogs charge to the opposite line and the catcher must try to touch as many bulldogs as possible. The bulldogs who get touched by the catcher become catchers for the next round. The winner is the last bulldog left.

Chicken

Play catch with a water balloon.

Spider race

It's a race on all fours – the catch is you're upside-down with your faces towards the sky.

Newspaper race

Each happy camper is given two sheets of newspaper. They must then place one of these sheets on the ground and step on it with one foot, then put the other piece down and step on that with the other foot. Once the second foot is down, the first can be lifted and the sheet of newspaper moved a step in front; the process is repeated in a race to a given line and back, with players allowed to step only on their newspaper.

The walnut game

This is a very funny game to watch, especially if you can get your dad doing it. You will need: two belts, two spoons, two whole walnuts in their shells, some string and two teams.

Decide which person on both teams is to go first. Fasten a belt around their waist and attach some string to the buckle. They must now bend their knees while the dangling end of the string is cut where it touches the ground. Next tie the hanging end of each bit of string to a spoon handle, making sure the spoon is facing forwards. Once attached, the spoons should not touch the floor unless the players are bending their legs.

To play, place the walnuts on a starting line in front of the first players. The players must then move the walnuts along using only their spoons, thus making very funny gyrating movements. The aim is for every walnutter to get their walnut to a set point and back before passing the belt to the next player, relay style. The winning team is the first to finish.

Swat

This is great to play on a lazy Sunday after you've eaten your scrambled eggs and completed the crossword. You will need two happy campers, two blindfolds, two rolled-up newspapers and a stick about half a metre in length.

The two players are first blindfolded and must then grab hold of opposite ends of the stick. They must hold the stick for the entire game; if they let go they will be disqualified. In their other hand they should hold the rolled-up newspaper and use it to swat their opponent on the head (swats to any other body parts are disallowed). The first person to land a fair swat wins the round; it's best of three and the winner stays on.

Horseshoes

This game is from our friend Dylan's dad, Irish Mick. He taught it to us when we went over to Ireland for his wedding; we all became addicted and played it the whole weekend.

You will need a set of four horseshoes (two horseshoes per team), two teams of two people, and two stakes (one per team).

Object of the game:

The idea is to throw the horseshoes to land as close as possible to the stake, so scoring the highest number of points.

How to play:

The first person to play for each team takes a shot, a nice underarm swing that gets the shoe spinning through the air towards the stake. Once they've had a shot with both horseshoes it's the next player's turn; players should keep taking turns for as long as everyone's happy to play – the winning team is the one which has scored the most points by the end of the game.

You score:

- Three points for a ringer: the horseshoe lands around the stake; the ends must pass the stake for the shot to count as a ringer.
- One point for a shoe's distance: the horseshoe lands within a width of a horseshoe (roughly fifteen centimetres/six inches) to the stake – we measure by putting another horseshoe between the stake and the shoe that's just been thrown.
- One point for a leaner: the horseshoe leans against the stake.

Take it in turns to pitch, which ever team scores the most points wins.

Cowboys and Indians

Get everyone to stand arm's-width apart in a circle; these are the cowboys. One person is elected the Indian and must jog around the outside of the circle. The Indian shouts out the name of somebody in the circle. That person then has to duck and the people either side of them must try to 'shoot' him (obviously, this is with their hands). If the person manages to duck in time and not get shot, the two either side will either shoot each other or one will be quicker and shoot the other. Whoever gets shot is out and the circle gets smaller. The winner is the last cowboy standing.

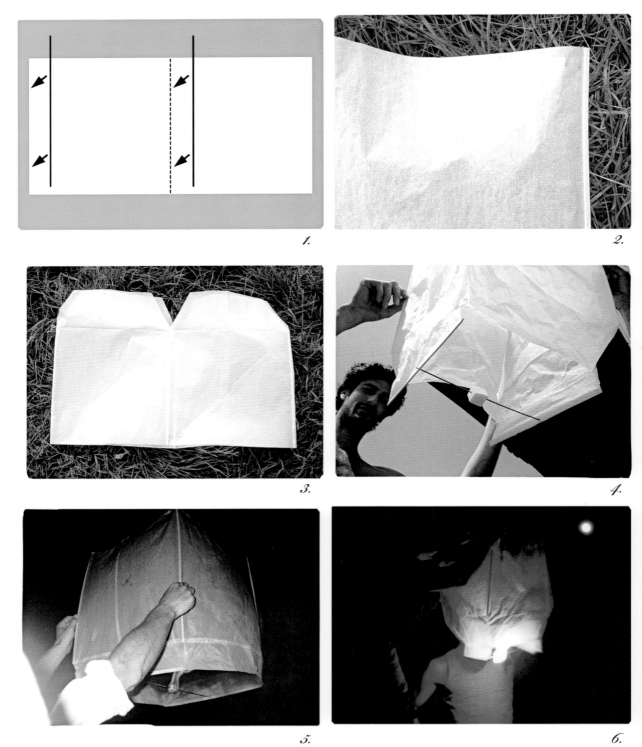

1.

2.

3.

4.

5.

6.

Hot air balloons by Karn and Terry

These look amazing set off on a calm night floating gently through the night sky till they self combust in a blaze of glory. Terry, Karn's dad, went to a party in Wales and they had a hot-air-balloon-making competition. They got into four groups and all had to produce one. Terry being a craftsman and very particular took ages, but his was the only one to go the distance, whereas all the others crashed and burned. There are two main things to remember – always set them off in very calm conditions or else all your hard work and patience will go to waste and be gentle when making your hot air balloon.

You will need:

    A packet of tissue paper
    Balsa wood (2mm x 4mm approx and needs to be in lengths of over 50cm)
    PVA glue (when using PVA be very sparing and use only very small amounts)
    Wire coat hanger
    Sharp scalpel
    Ruler
    Patience, a sunny day to make it, a very calm night to set it off, lots of people
      to watch

Step 1. Cut out 2 pieces of tissue paper, size 50cm x 100cm, and fold them in half along the longest side to make a square. Cut 4 pieces of balsa wood at 50cm long. Take one of the pieces of tissue paper and glue one strip of balsa wood along a short edge. Glue another strip of balsa along the folded line (see figs. 1 and 2). Do the same with the second piece of paper.

Step 2. Glue both pieces together to form a 4-sided box (see fig.3).

Step 3. For the roof, cut out a square of tissue paper 51cm x 51cm and gently glue on.

Step 4. For the tapered skirt of the balloon which keeps the hot air in. Create a piece of tissue paper 200cm x 10cm (you will need to join tissue paper together). At each 50cm cut a 'V' shape out (see fig. 3) and affix to the bottom of the balloon, glueing the 'V' shapes together as you go.

Step 5. Reinforce 2 sides of the skirt using balsa wood strips (see fig. 4).

Step 6. Cut a piece of wire from your coat hanger 20cm longer than the opening. Cut a firelighter into thirds and thread one piece onto the wire. Then push the wire through the balsa wood strips that reinforce the skirt (see fig. 5). The balloon is now ready to fly.

To set off your balloon you will need two people to hold opposite corners of the balloon while the firelighter is lit. Wait till you feel the balloon fill with hot air and it getting lighter. Gently release and watch in wonder.

Back to simple

Make grass squeal
You can make grass squeal by tickling it . . . Well, not really, but you can really impress your friends with this simple trick: pick a thick, shiny blade of grass; press it between the sides of your thumbs so that you can see its edge, stretch it nice and tight and blow through the hole left by your thumbs.

Blow some bubbles
Use some wire or a paperclip to form a circle with a handle. Mix up some bubble potion (washing-up liquid and a little water). Dip in your blower and blow gently till a bubble floats away.

Make a windmill
You will need some thin card, a map pin, a small piece of cork, a stick, a pen and a straight edge. Draw a square on the card. Draw lines from the corners, leaving a space in the middle (see diagram). Cut down the lines and fold each corner to the centre, fastening them with the pin. Secure the pin to a stick, first putting the cork in between the stick and the windmill so that it spins easily.

Sardines
Someone is a sardine. Everyone else closes their eyes and slowly counts to 100 while the sardine hides. Then everyone searches for the sardine. When a person finds the sardine they must hide with it and become a sardine too. The loser is the last person to find the sardines. This is great to play where there are lots of hiding places, such as on sand dunes, in woods and on busy campsites. Note: not brilliant to play at festivals as you risk losing your friends.

Homemade postcards
Spread the love; send a homemade postcard.

We don't need to tell you how to . . .
Play leapfrog.
Make a daisy chain.
Look for a four-leaf clover.
Bury your friends in the sand.
Play rounders.
Make sandcastles – then jump on them.
Play hide-and-seek.
Write message in the sand or with sticks.
Make a den.
Play kiss chase.

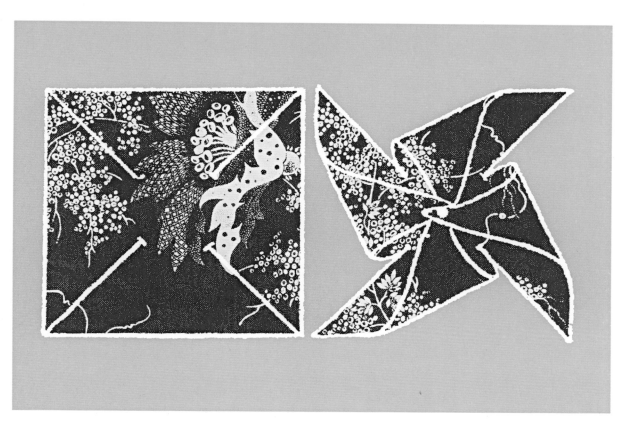

Indian headdress

You will need a variety of feathers,
a length of ribbon and
a needle and thread.

1   Tie the ribbon around your head and make a faint
    mark with a pen by the knot, then untie.
2   Leaving a little space between each feather, sew them
    tightly on to the ribbon up to the marks you made.
3   To put on your headdress, tip your head forward and place
    the centre of the ribbon on your forehead. Tie the ribbon
    in a bow at the back of your head. Lift your head et voilà!
4   Have a pow wow (optional).

Dylan's simple bow and arrow

You will need:

A sharp knife or saw

A straight length of hazel-wood branch for your bow, about 1.5m long and 2.5cm thick

Some smaller lengths of hazel, for arrows, about 50cm long and 1.5cm thick

Strong string

Feathers, for flights (one for each arrow) – they should be quite symmetrical

Waterproof (electrical or insulation) tape

Making the bow:

1   Hopefully you'll have found a nice straight bit of hazel for your bow, a branch that doesn't taper too much so both ends are roughly the same thickness (fig. 1). Cut it to length and trim off any excess twigs and leaves.

2   Bend the branch over your knee to find its natural bending direction.

3   Cut small notches in both ends of the branch to prevent the string slipping when you tie it on. The notches should be in the same direction as the natural bend of the bow. Bind ends with string to prevent branch splitting (fig. 2).

4   Take one end of your string and place it firmly into the slots at one end of the bow. Then wind the string around the end of the bow, making sure you pass under as well as over the bow string (fig. 2). Tie a knot every so often. Keep winding until you feel you have a secure string that isn't going to slip. Finish by tying more knots.

5   Now turn the branch the other way round, get hold of the string and use your knee to bend the bow. As you do so place the loose end of the string in the slots on the branch and tightly wind around the end of the stick as before (fig. 3). You should now have a simple bow (fig. 4).

Making arrows:

1   Remove the bark and any notches from your smaller pieces of hazel.

2   Place an arrow stick across the bow to get a feel for how long your arrows need to be. They should protrude about 15cm past the bow when at full stretch. Cut your small branches to length.

3   Look down the length of each arrow and counter-bend any wobbles you can see.

4   Now prepare your flights by cutting off any excess feather and leaving the stems to be taped in place (fig. 5). Put a feather on one of your arrows, leaving a space of about 3cm from the end to allow for grip, then tape securely at both ends. Repeat with each arrow.

5   Next carefully cut a groove for the bow-string in the end of each arrow. This should run in the same direction as the feather.

6   Finally, sharpen the end of your arrows and there you go – a bunch of arrows that should fly pretty straight. Stand back, admire your work and feel proud (fig. 6).

Shoot an arrow, tied to a rope, over a tree branch to make a rope swing.

love Dylan x

1.

2.

3.

4.

5.

6.

Water babies

If you're lucky enough to be camping near the sea, a river or lake don't forget to:

- Skim some stones.
- Find a natural slide in the rocks.
- Play pooh-sticks.
- Fish for minnows.
- Make yourself a seaweed beard.
- Go swimming with flippers on to make you speedy.
- Practise handstands in the water.
- Play water 'it': in waist-high water, one person is 'it' and must try to catch the others by touching them. When someone is caught they must hold hands with the 'it' and become an 'it' as well. This continues and the line of 'its' gets longer. The winner is the last person still free.
- Go snorkelling.
- Take a waterproof camera and go looking for sharks.
- Go body surfing.
- Go crabbing.
- Just float and enjoy the peace.

Seaside games

Sandy-beach Olympics

In fact you can play your Olympics anywhere but sand does help with any hard landings. Things can get very competitive, so it's a good idea to decide on an adjudicator whose decision is final.

Try the following activities: sumo wrestling; long jump; gymnastics; high jump; 30-metre dash; 25-metre doggy paddle; shot put (using a rock); javelin (using a long stick).

Tips:

Have plenty of water to hand and some oranges for half time.

Don't play against Karn – he always wins.

Beach tennis

Almost any number of people can play – just divide yourselves into two teams. Mark out the court, a rectangle 4.5m x 9m divided into three equal widths. The teams must position themselves in the two end rectangles and use their hands to bat an inflatable ball to each other across the centre rectangle. Points are gained when the opposing team knocks the ball out of court or lets it fall in the middle rectangle during play.

Make angels in the sand

Lie down on your back in the sand and move your arms up and down and your legs in and out.

Beach acrobatics

The beach is a great place to test your circus skills. Make a human pyramid or try standing on your boyfriend's/girlfriend's/dad's/aunty's shoulders.

Beach volleyball

There is always a lot of debate about the rules of beach volleyball, so here is our simplified version.

1 Set up the net – about 2.5m high. Mark out the court: a rectangle measuring 18m x 9m.

2 You should have an equal number of players on each team (ideally five aside). The teams must stand on opposite sides of the net; players should then position themselves like a five on a dice i.e. Four forming a square with one in the centre. Players rotate position by one place for every serve, so there's a new server each time.

3 The object of the game is to get the ball over the net using your hands or wrists without it touching the floor.

4 When the ball is in play, a team is allowed a maximum of three passes before the ball goes over the net – so two passes between team mates and one pass to send the ball over the net.

5 To decide which team will serve first, pass the ball over the net three times and then start play. The team that wins the point gets first serve.

6 The server always stands on the right-hand side of the back line and hits the ball over the net to start the game. The ball must go over the net on the first attempt; if it doesn't, the player loses his turn and the other team serve.

7 Teams win a point when the ball touches the ground on the opposite side of the net, and when the opposing team hits the ball out of court. However you score points only when your team is serving. If your team concedes a point during play following their serve, serve switches to the other team.

8 The first team to score twenty-one points wins the match.

. . . **just go for a walk**

Recipe for making boys happy

You will need:

> One hacky sack
> A flattish piece of ground
> A sunny day and some boys (though girls can play too – there's no discrimination in hacky)

Hacky is a game best played in a group but you can practise on your own. It's portable, which is why it's perfect for happy camping. The players stand in a circle and do tricks with the hacky sack while passing it around. The idea is that everyone in the circle gets to touch the hacky sack at least once. That is called 'getting a hacky'. The hacky sack (sometimes called a footbag) can be made out of a variety of materials, from leather to crocheted cotton, and is filled with plastic pellets, lentils or even sand. The hacky behaves differently depending on what and how much filling has been used: the less filling it has the slower and squishier it is, which makes it easier to play with.

The basic rules:

- You serve by throwing the hacky towards the feet of anyone you choose in the circle.
- Never self-serve.
- Don't use your hands or arms except when serving. Shoulders are generally allowed and can lead to some great tricks.
- Never, ever say sorry – everyone makes mistakes!

Some hacky-sack tricks:

- Toe stall: stop the hacky on the top of your foot.
- Inside/outside stall: stop the hacky on the inside or outside of your foot.
- Around-the-world: everyone in the group kicks the hacky around the outside of the circle.
- Around-the-hacky: circle the bag with your foot between toe kicks.
- Blind scorpion: blindly kick, behind you, sending the hacky sack forward over your head again.
- Crouching tiger: catch the hacky between your thighs in a sitting position; then drop it through your legs and kick, if you can.
- Swinger: stall the hacky on your toe, then bring your leg straight back and launch the hacky over your head into play.
- Pop off: catch the hacky in the back of your knee; then turn round and fully and forcefully extend your leg to pop the hacky back into the circle.

Note: we made up these names for the tricks – see what others you can come up with.

Taking photos

Everyone loves a photo. There's something really magical about being able to capture memories on paper so you can look back at them and fondly reminisce. We're addicted to snapping every single moment we can: happy holidays, secret passions, random flashes, lives lived, blurred nothings, unusual angles, beautiful friends – simply everything, just to get our hearts pounding when we pick up that crisp envelope of prints from the developers.

The majority of the photos in this book are our own and they have been taken on a really simple camera, a lomo. We discovered this little gem about six years ago and haven't been able to put it down since. One of the reasons why we love it is its auto light function, which makes it possible to shoot photographs in almost complete darkness without the need for a flash. But that isn't the only thing that makes the lomo unique. Its specially developed wide-angle lens delivers super-sharp images in intensely concentrated colours. The lens is also slightly curved, creating real-life depth and darkening the corners (vignetting), resulting in beautifully framed shots. The lomo has become a bit of a cult acquisition, with an online community of thousands of 'lomographers' from all over the world all sharing their photos, tips and tricks.

Even though we are living in a digital age, traditional cameras remain as popular as ever. Part of their appeal lies in the not knowing what you've captured and embracing the unpredictable and often surprising results. We're not suggesting you rush out and buy a lomo today – any old print camera will do; just experiment and have fun.

Our photos were part of the inspiration for this book. We wanted to be able to share some of our special memories and show how easy it is to create your own deliciously nostalgic images.

Embrace the movement

Don't worry if you have a bit of camera shake – movement and blurring can help the image come alive. You can even take advantage of this and deliberately move the camera as you snap your pictures.

Try following your moving subject (person, dog, seagull) as you take the shot so that it is static and the background is blurred.

Or try setting the focus slightly off to lend your images a hazy quality.

Nostalgia

For that 1970s look, try putting your used roll of undeveloped film in your trouser pocket in a 40°c wash, and then get it processed. Or buy some skin-tone stockings, stretch one over your camera lens and click away.

. . . more tips

Cross-processing

To get photos that are bursting with saturated colour and contrast use a slide film in your camera and get it developed as if it were a print film. You should be able to get this done at any friendly high-street processing lab. A bright sunny day is the most favourable time for taking pictures to be cross-processed, but taking them at dusk or dawn will get you more atmospheric results. Your end product will vary from film brand to film brand and lab to lab, so it is hard to predict what you will get, but this just makes it even more exciting.

Double exposure

Very slowly rewind your film; as soon as you feel the pressure release, stop rewinding so a little tongue of the film is left out of the canister. Then just reload the film again and snap away. Get your prints processed as normal for a double exposure of weird and wonderful images.

Underwater love

Buy a cheap waterproof camera and go snapping in river, lido, lake or sea to catch some underwater action.

Play with light

If your camera has a manual shutter, decrease its speed to let in more light to achieve interesting night-time effects. If your camera has an external light meter, like the lomo, simply cover it with your finger as you're taking a picture to keep the shutter open for longer.

Point your camera at a light source and slowly move it around, creating fuzzy masses of light.

Or try holding it still to photograph moving light to create dazzling pictures of streaming luminosity; in this way you can capture the sparks of the campfire. Also try it with passing cars, using your dashboard as a tripod, or get someone to write or draw a shape with a torch or penlight as you keep the shutter open revealing secret messages burnt straight on to the film.

'*Let the rain kiss you. Let the rain beat upon your head with silver beads, let the rain sing you a lullaby.*'
Langston Hughes

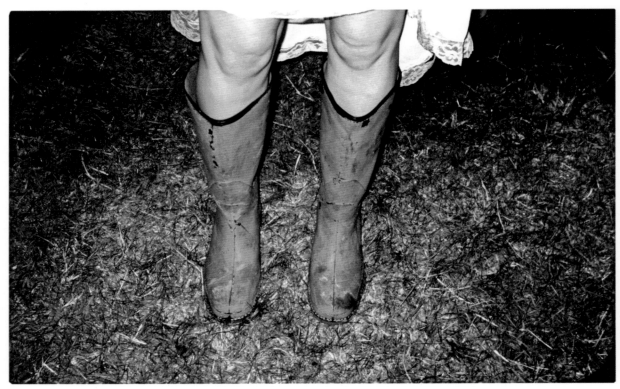

Wet-weather days

- Visit a museum, art gallery, exhibition or other local attraction.
- Go surfing, swimming, canoeing or just play in a river – you're going to get wet anyway.
- Make yourself a face pack (see page 257) and kick back in your tent with a mate setting the world to rights.
- Play card games.
- Get a game of poker on the go with brandy and brownies as refreshments.
- Go streaking.
- Do some mud-wrestling.
- Make a kite for when the rain clears (see page 173).
- Go back to bed – it is undeniably one of the loveliest things to do, being tucked away in your tent with your loved one/ones, the pitter-patter of the rain on your tent as you drift off back to sleep.
- Play spin the bottle in your tent.
- Go to the pub. One memorable trip of ours included a row-boat ride to a cosy pub where we spent the afternoon beside a crackling open fire with pints of the black stuff and boardgames.
- Knit a scarf (see page 206).
- Play lots of chinese checkers (see page 204).
- Eat lots.
- Have a wet-T-shirt competition.
- Play monopoly.
- Go to the local cream-tea or coffee shop, get the paper, do the crossword and see what's on locally.
- Play welly wanging.
- Put on your waterproofs and go for a walk, then reward yourself by ending up at the pub or a restaurant for some food.
- Go and get some fish and chips, drive to a beautiful view and eat them in the car looking at said beautiful view.
- Go mushrooming, if they are in season – they love the wet weather.
- Go to the nearest cinema and catch a matinee.
- Go fishing or frog spotting.
- If it's really chucking it down, and has been for the last three days or more, treat yourselves to a B&B and a hot bath.
- Go shopping.
- Go to a theme park with water slides – again, you're going to get wet anyway, and the queues will be much shorter.
- Play charades in your tent.
- Have a water fight.

Chinese checkers

We're addicted!

Chinese checkers is a game for two, three, four or six people. For the six-player game all six points of the star are used. If there are two players, play starts in opposing triangles; a four-player game starts in two pairs of opposing triangles. In a three-player game the pegs will start in three equidistant triangles.

Each player has ten counters, which are placed on the corresponding coloured spaces in each of the six points of the star. To use our board, you will need to make your own counters. The best method we've found is to use little balls of blu-tack with either coloured drawing pins stuck in or circles of coloured paper attached (raid magazines for lots of colours). This stops your counters going for a walk, a bit like an antiquated version of a magnetic travel game.

You need a maximum of six sets of ten counters in different colours.

Object of the game:

To get all your counters across the board and into the star point directly opposite your starting point. The first player to occupy all ten destination spaces is the winner.

How to play:

Players take turns to move a single counter of their own colour. In one turn a counter may either be simply moved into an adjacent hole or it may make one or more jumps over other counters. When a jump is made it must be over an adjacent counter (of any colour) and into the vacant space directly beyond it. If possible the player may make an unlimited amount of jumps. (So it is possible to move a counter from the starting triangle right across the board and into the opposite triangle in just one turn.) The players may move or jump in any direction as long as they follow the lines. Players can use any space in the hexagon, but cannot use spaces within the points of the star other than their starting and destination points.

How to knit a scarf *

Knitting a scarf is simpler than you'd think. In fact it's really easy once you're actually knitting – you just keep going until it's long enough. The secret to making a scarf in no time at all is big thick wool and big thick needles. Neither of us are accomplished knitters but we both managed to knit ourselves a lovely warm scarf in a day or two. You will need two big (20mm) needles and two to three balls of very chunky wool.

Casting on
1   Make a slip knot with the wool and place on a needle and hold in your left hand, hold the empty needle in your right hand.
2   Place the right-hand needle into the loop underneath the left-hand needle.
3   With your right hand bring the wool under and over the point of the right-hand needle.
4   Bring the right-hand needle towards you and draw the wool through the stitch with the needle point to make a new stitch.
5   Loop the stitch onto the left-hand needle (don't pull the stitch too tight). Continue making these loops until you have fourteen stitches on the needle.

Plain knitting
6   Hold the needle with the stitches in your left hand and the empty needle in your right hand.
7–9 Same as in casting on (2–4).
10   Slide the old stitch off the left needle. Continue to the end of the row.
11   Once you have transferred all the knitting to the right-hand needle, turn the work round so that the needle holding the stitches is in your left hand. Start the next row.
12   Keep knitting like this until you have used up nearly all of the wool (you will need to leave some spare to cast off) or until you decide your scarf is long enough.

Casting off
13   Knit two stitches on to the right-hand needle.
14   Put the point of your left-hand needle into the first of these stitches.
15   Hold the excess wool around the index finger on your right hand. Take the stitch over the second stitch you just knitted and slide it off both needles. You should now have one stitch on your right-hand needle.
16   Knit one stitch so that you once again have two stitches on the right-hand needle. Repeat the process until you have only one last stitch left. Break off the wool, pass the end through the stitch and pull tight. Attach tassels if you fancy.

*Alternatively, grab a granny and get her to show you how to do it.

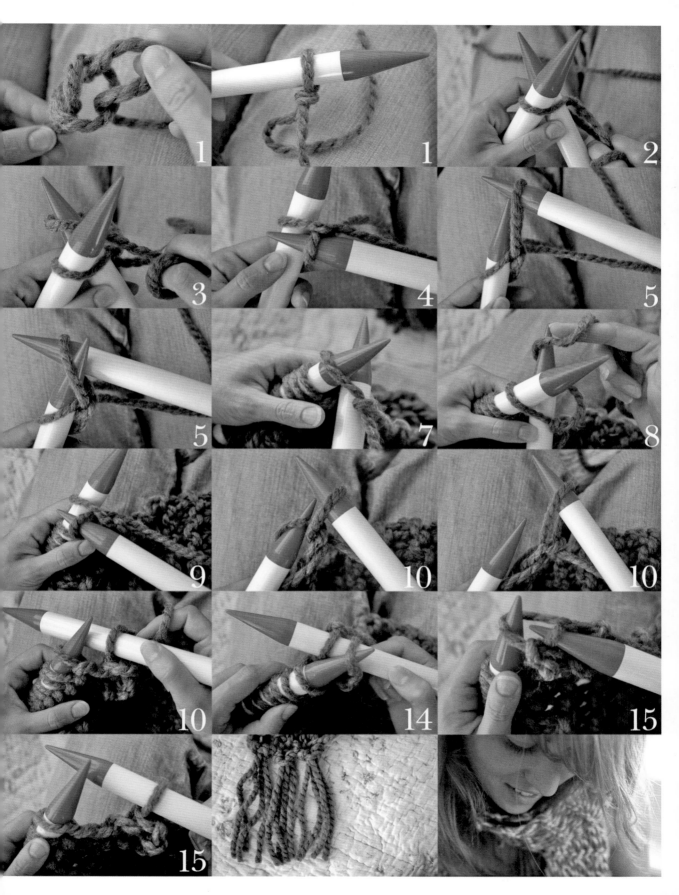

There's treasure in them there hills

When we were kids Mama Carr was famous for her birthday parties because of her treasure hunts, which the parents loved too because their kids would go home happy but completely exhausted. We still love a good treasure hunt, especially when Tess is instigating it with the promise of liquid refreshment.

The rum trail treasure hunt

For up to twenty adult players. You can do some preparation for this at home.

First, decide how many clues you're going to make – about ten is a good amount. Decide on a theme; in this instance it's pirates. Draw a template of a bottle (or other simple shape related to your theme). Using your template, you're now going to cut out a number of paper shapes; to get your total, multiply the number of clues you've decided on by the number of players or pairs of players you'll have – so if you'll have ten clues and twenty treasure hunters working in pairs you will need to cut out 100 bottles. So do keep the template really simple and cut through a few pieces of paper at a time.

Now divide your shapes into as many piles as you have clues (ten clues equals ten piles) and number them: each bottle on the first pile is '1'; each bottle on the second pile is '2'; and so on. Then put each pile of bottles into its own plastic bag.

Don't forget the treasure – a bottle or two of rum (or your favourite tipple) and enough cups for everyone.

When you're set up at camp, find a place in which to hide each bag of bottles and a place in which to hide the treasure. (This bit is more fun if you have a helper.) Now for the tricky part: you need to write the clues that will direct the players to each bag plus one final clue to lead them to the treasure. Your clues can be as easy, hard or cryptic as you like, depending on how long you want the game to go on for; they should all be written down on separate pieces of paper.

When it's time to start the hunt, give each player or pair of players a different clue to read. Once they've read it they must go in search of the bags of bottles. They must bring a bottle from the bag to you before they'll get a new clue. The first player or pair of players to collect a bottle from every bag wins the final clue, leading to the treasure: the real bottle of booze, which will keep them and all the other hunters happy for a whole evening around the campfire.

Kids' treasure hunts

This is a very simple yet effective way to keep the kids entertained for hours while you relax in the sun. Its beauty lies in the fact that there is very little preparation necessary. It works really well on the beach, as you can keep an eye on your little hunters, but can be played just as easily elsewhere.

Fill a bag with enough treasure for all the participating children (enough treasure equals no tears). Then make a list of objects that can be found fairly easily – for example, if you're on the beach you could include a pebble, a shell, a seagull feather, a piece of seaweed, etc., or if you're in the woods a fir cone, a conker, a certain leaf, etc. Send the children off either individually or in pairs to find an item. When they return with the item give them another thing to find from the list. Meanwhile, read your book, relax, have a glass of wine.

The first child to find all the objects gets first dip in the bag of treasure.

Alternatively, get your kids to devise a treasure hunt for you to do at the end of the day; this too will keep them entertained for hours.

The dressing-up box

We are the queens of dressing up and love to rope everyone else into our favourite pastime. Sometimes we pack the dressing-up box to take camping with us so that everyone can help themselves when the mood strikes. Some people protest but it doesn't take them long to give in and fashion themselves some fantastic outfit; such protesters are usually boys and they almost always end up in a dress.

The dressing-up game

This is a game for two players; the winner stays on if there are enough of you keen to play.

Get a big pile, box or basketful of clothes. Two players face off over the box. When the elected games master shouts 'dress!' the players have to frantically put on as many garments from the box as possible. The fact that there is only one box of clothes could lead to fisticuffs over the more desirable items, but all's fair in love and dressing-up games.

When the box is empty and the players are considerably fatter than when they started, the game is over. They then have to take it turns to peel off the layers of clothes while the games master counts how many items they put on. You can get them to undress striptease-style and judge that too. The winner is the player who was wearing the most items.

Dressing-up relay

Divide into two equal teams and make two piles of dressing-up clothes in front of the teams. Put similar garments on both piles, so you get a fair race. When the race starts, the first contestant for each team has to put on all the clothes from their team's pile, leg it to a designated point and back and then take all the clothes off. The next player can start putting the clothes as the other player is taking them off; and then runs the same course. Play continues like this until all the players have run the course. The winning team is the first to finish.

Just get dressed up

There's always a reason to celebrate when camping, whether it's a birthday, an engagement or just that somebody's finished the washing up. Dressing up is a great way to put everyone in the party mood. It does lead to a few stares at camp, but this adds to the fun. Why not have a theme?

- A mad hatter's tea party
- Cowboys and Indians
- Charity-shop chic (a good impromptu dress-up, as you can raid the local charity shops)
- Speedos and swimsuits
- Bearded ladies
- Ramblers

Camping piñata

Big Ad's piñatas are legendary. Piñatas are a Mexican tradition and have since become one of our camping traditions. They are great fun for everybody and help to release a bit of pent-up fury over who isn't contributing to camp chores. You're meant to make them out of papier-mâché but obviously when you're camping this is a bit tricky. So we have devised a simple way of making one that uses what you might have to hand at camp.

1   Get an old cardboard box and fill it with leaves, grass, twigs, etc.
2   Add some wrapped sweets or chocolates and tape up the box. The more securely you tape it, the longer the game will last.
3   Wrap the box up like a present, if you have any wrapping paper.
4   Attach a rope securely around the box.

To play:

Find a suitable branch, a metre or so above head height, and throw the rope over it. Assign a rope master who will hold on to the end of the rope and control the height of the box. Find a piñata-hitting implement – a big stick, a mallet, a wooden leg, or something. The first player must equip themselves with the weapon of their choice and don a blindfold (use long socks). All the other campers gather round, drinks in hand (as all the shouting will leave your throats a bit parched). The rope master must pull the piñata above the player's head to start the game. The player has to whack the piñata to release the sweets. The gathered campers help the player by shouting 'left a bit, right a bit', etc. The rope master can make the task more difficult by pulling the piñata up and down to disorientate the player, who often hits nothing more than thin air.

After a few minutes another player takes a turn. Play continue like this until the piñata is defeated, bursting open and showering the sweets on to the ground – at which point there is a mass pile-on to get to the booty.

Note: this can be a very noisy game so consider your neighbours or invite them to join in. And always pick up all the sweets and wrappers.

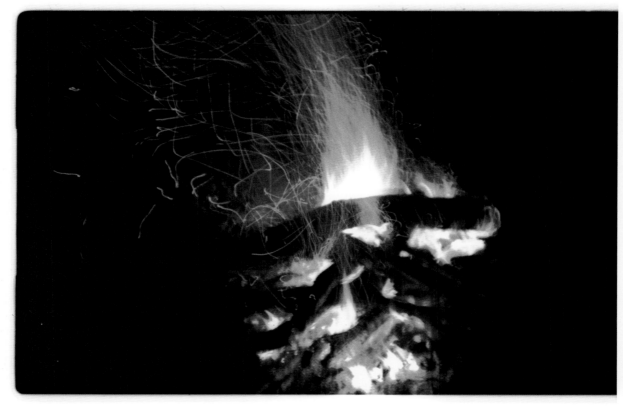

Around the campfire

Storytelling

There is definitely an art to storytelling. Some people are naturally good at it while others just need a little practice. It does help if you're a bit of a show-off, but the main thing is to try to create an atmosphere.

- Add little details such as the colour of a dress, the feeling of someone watching you, the smell of fear.
- Vary the volume and tone of your voice – be quiet and whispery for extra spookiness and screech unexpectedly to make your audience jump.
- Make sound effects – a howling wind, a hooting owl or a bloodcurdling scream.
- Give your listeners objects with which to create a sound whenever you say a specific word.
- Give the characters distinctive voices.
- Use your hands to help describe the scene.
- Change your focus from one person to the next, always making eye contact.

Lies, all lies

Learn more about your fellow campers. Take it in turns to make three statements of which two are true and one is a lie. See if anyone can guess which one is the lie.

Murder in the winks

Cut or tear some scraps of paper – one for each person. On one piece write 'murderer'; the other pieces should remain blank. Fold up the bits of paper and shuffle them together. Each person must take a piece of paper and looking at it without showing the others. The person with 'murderer' written on their paper is the murderer and must try sneakily to wink at the other campers in turn. When someone is winked at they must keel over and die (cue unconvincing dying noises). If the murderer is caught winking by someone other than their victim, they have lost and the game is over.

Who am I?

Each person takes a small piece of paper and on it writes the name of someone famous (living or dead) before sticking the piece of paper to the forehead of the person next to them. Take it in turns to ask questions to find out who you are. You can ask only one question at a time and the other players can answer only 'yes' or 'no'. Keep going until everyone guesses who they are.

Games to play after dark

Torchlight tag

This works best on cloudy or moonless nights. Decide on a play area – the larger the area the more difficult the game. The catcher has a torch and must chase after the other players in the dark. Each time a person is caught they must return to base; the winner is the last person left free.

Tent sardines

You need lots of tents for this one. Restrict everyone to crawling on all fours to avoid tripping over guy ropes and tent pegs.

Elect a sardine. While everyone else closes their eyes and slowly counts to 100 the sardine goes to hide in one of the tents and there attempt to disguise themselves as a rucksack or something. When the counting's up it's time for everyone else to go sardine hunting. Anyone who spots the sardine mustn't give away their hiding place but should wait until no one is looking before quietly slipping in and hiding with the sardine. Try to suppress giggles as they will definitely lead to you being found out. Eventually everyone disappears leaving the loser, who must make everyone brandy coffee.

Night-time hide and seek

A base is agreed and the seeker counts to fifty while the others hide. The players must try to reach the base without being seen. If the seeker sees you and calls your name before you reach base, you're out. Try switching clothes to fool the seeker.

Fireflies

Agree on your playing area – don't make it too large or you'll get lost. The person elected firefly carries a torch and runs off into the woods, fields or whatever to hide. When they're ready they must flash the torch twice. The rest of the players count to fifty and then pursue the firefly. The firefly should evade capture for as long as possible by hiding and changing direction but must flash the torch once a minute. The winner is the person who catches the firefly.

Murder in the socks

We made up this version of murder in the dark when we were kids and it's still great fun when the mood is silly. Play in a field or around your camp area – it does need to be properly dark, though, so won't really work if you have a fire lit.

All the players must wear socks (no cheating by wearing multiple pairs). Everyone crawls around feeling for socks in the dark and nicking them off people's feet as they go. The minute someone loses both socks they must freeze, creating an obstacle for the remaining players. This continues until only the winner remains triumphant with at least one sock intact.

Glow-stick football

Play football in the dark – attach glow-sticks to your feet, the football and the goal markers.

Night walking

Why not go for a night walk and see the world from a different perspective? Don't switch the torch on – if you let your eyes adjust to the darkness you'll be much more likely to see some nocturnal wildlife. Night walking can be really beautiful when the moon is full, casting a soft light and making everything sparkle. Water looks especially amazing under a moonlit sky, so stroll along the beach or riverbank and try not to fall in!

wild world

The happy-camping seasons

A couple of years ago, while waiting for winter to leave and spring to arrive, we decided to help the process along a bit so bravely packed up the tents and went to Wales. The sun was shining but it was still cold so we wore a million layers and packed plenty of duvets, blankets and hot-water bottles. It was one of the most magical camps we've been on. The landscape we'd thought was sleeping soundly was actually showing tentative signs of waking up. The air was filled with the love songs of birds trying to attract a new mate, buds and hanging catkins bejewelled the trees and tiny lambs dotted the fields. Over the winter we had become so citified we had forgotten how early spring sprung.

Camping at any time of year is a great way of letting the outside in but during the change of season it couldn't be more so. The signs are everywhere – just open your eyes a little wider.

Spring

Spring is a time of gathering excitement as the days suddenly get longer and the promise of new adventures abound.

The return of greenery

Flowering starts with the crocus, followed by clusters of snowdrops, primroses and sunny daffodils.

Buds and catkins appear on many trees. Look out for yellow hazel catkins; in olden days hazel was thought to be a magic plant and its sticks used for divining rods.

In city parks oriental cherry blossom trickles down like confetti almost as soon as it's out, hinting at what's going on in the countryside on blossoming crab apple and wild cherry trees.

In damp places the male fern unfurls its gold-green fronds. Bracken fern spreads its way over heath land.

Star-shaped yellow celandine, white wood anemone and pink-veined wood sorrel make a patchwork carpet in woodlands.

Cow parsley plants appear in every roadside hedgerow.

Towards the end of spring the focus shifts from woodland to meadow; cuckoo flower, herb robert and meadow vetchling with its distinctive curled tendrils spring up, soon joined by pretty yellow cowslips and masses of dandelions.

Bluebells appear en masse and woods shimmer with colour. The bell-shaped deep-blue flowers can be found all over the country but cast a particularly spectacular shade of blue in ancient oak and beech woods from April through to May. You can find your nearest bluebell wood on the internet. Look out for the telltale crisscrossed paths left by snuffling badgers and don't forget to be nice to the bluebells themselves – they're an endangered species, so try not to tread on them.

A little later the lush green and white of wild garlic emerges.

Spring wildlife

- Frogs spawn appears in ponds and bogs. Deeper down is toad spawn, floating pearl-like strings.
- March hares go a little mad about their love affairs.
- Cuckoos call out their own name and ladybirds emerge from hibernation.
- Bumblebees feed on sweet clover and the bright pink ragged robin.
- Swallows, with their forked tails and long streamers, flit about the sky chasing swifts who spend their lives on the wing. Swifts used to be known as demon birds, because they were thought to look like packs of demons screaming and dashing through the sky.
- Orange tip, swallowtail, peacock, brimstone and green hairstreak butterflies are coaxed out of hibernation by the faintest hint of warmth.
- Cuckoo spit, a protective white froth produced by young insects called froghoppers, sits on plants while dragonflies clamber out of the water and hatch as flying adults in late spring.

The dawn chorus pipes up before sunrise with just one or two birds singing. It usually starts with the blackbird, followed by the song thrush, wren, robin, great tit and chaffinch. Gradually they are joined by more species of birds – among them the whinchat, meadow pipit and dunnock – until, by mid-morning, there is a rousing symphony to greet you from your lie in.

It's quite hard to describe bird calls but once you've identified them it's easier to remember than you'd think and it's nice to know who your neighbours are.

It might help to whistle the following to yourself: *
Song thrush
The song thrush repeats his clear, flute-like call three or four times:
(peepeep)(peepeep)(peepeep) – (whoeeeoo)(whoeeeoo)(whoeeeoo)

Blackbird

During the winter blackbirds like to hum quietly to themselves in the undergrowth but in spring and early summer they take up a perch and belt out a sweet, melodious song. There's is a sound you will have heard before; so once you've named that tune it'll be easy to remember. The song is a series of three or four phrases, each ending in a little squawk. Each phrase is slightly different but seems to time quite well with 'four and twenty blackbirds':
(who)(eee)(who)(eee) – whooooeeeeee – (squawk)
(four)(and)(twen)(ty) – blackbirds – (squawk)

Meadow pipit

He sings his repetitive song while airborne. It is reminiscent of the noise of a firework – a steady, high-pitched (tseep tseep tseep tseep tseep) as he's flying up, then a little pause followed by (tseut tseut tseut tseut tseut), each one falling in pitch as he dives.

---

*( ) denotes a fast sound – signifies a short pause

Extra-nice things about camping in spring
The possibility of shedding our scarves and mittens.
You can put lemon-drizzled spring greens on top of warming soup.
It's a delight to sit out and feel the sun and fresh air on your centrally heated skin.
Everything looks fresh and green and hope is in the air.
The sun comes out and sometimes we even have to reach for the shade of the trees.
The scent of spring blooming all at once.
When the sun shines the buttercup says we all love butter.
More rainbows.
The campsites are empty.
You get home feeling like the winter has gone.

Summer

The verdant green and brilliant flowers of spring give way to the lovely untidiness of summer. Meadows go to seed, buttercups are overgrown by tall grass and the countryside takes on a misty air. Summer is the perfect season for camping: more often than not the weather is perfect and happy, long summer days stretch into balmy summer nights.

Hazy lazy days

- Wildflowers all but disappear, leaving just the trees to drift along serenely as green as ever.
- The horse chestnut is laden with huge leaves, giving welcome shade from the midday sun.
- The romantic dog rose appears in woods and hedgerows. This is also a great time to visit fragrant rose gardens.
- Sweet-smelling wild honeysuckle blooms in woods and hedgerows; the flowers are pollinated at night by moths.
- Daisies and dandelions gather force, carpeting any piece of grass they can.
- Wild-strawberry hunts are going on across the country.
- Cow parsley is replaced by the similar-shaped upturned flowers of chervil and smelly hogweed.
- On the way to another adventure we zoom past day-glow fields of oil seed rape.
- The hedgerows are alive with the aromas of marjoram, with its clumps of tiny pink flowers.
- Delicious marsh samphire spreads over seaside salt marshes also known as poor man's asparagus, samphire is a type of succulent found on the southeast and west coasts of England. You can pick samphire wild during July and August at low tide by cutting it with scissors just above the roots. Choose only the healthiest plants, those that will have been washed by every tide. If you don't fancy getting your hands mucky you can also find it alongside the fresh fish at the local fishmonger's or from roadside stalls run by resourceful kids during their summer holidays.
- By rivers or in damp places yellow flags grow, bulrushes and other waterside plants are tall and green, while white lilies float like delicate china cups.
- Teasels begin to lose their purple crowns, their brittle heads becoming food for the goldfinch; thistles produce fluffy clouds of star-shaped seeds that float on the breeze.
- Spikes of poisonous foxglove grow tall.

It is said that if you stand under an elder tree on midsummer's eve you will see Oberon, the king of the fairies, ride by.

Elder is found growing wild and free in woods and hedges flowers in June in large, flat plates of flower heads called umbels comprising many tiny cream-white flowers. If you make sure they are clean of bugs, they can be eaten straight off the branch on a hot summer's day (never eat the stems – they would give you an upset tummy).

Granny's non-alcoholic elderflower champagne

To make this elderflower cordial pick the flowers in full bloom on a dry, warm and sunny day. Don't pick flowers that are damaged or discoloured or near busy roadsides where they are exposed to traffic pollution. Don't wash them, so as to preserve their fragrance, but do examine and shake each head gently to remove any tiny unwanted guests.

> 20 flowerheads
> 30g (1oz) citric acid
> Juice of 2 lemons
> 450g (1lb) sugar
> 450g (1lb) brown sugar
> 1 litre (1³/₄ pints) boiling water

Mix the flowerheads, sugar, citric acid and lemon juice in a jug and pour over the boiling water. Cover and leave for four to five days. Strain and pour into clean bottles. Cork the next day and use as a cordial (it will keep for up to a year).

Under the summer sun wheat fields turn a darker gold, their edges dotted with red poppies. Root crops make a patchwork of blue, green and purple. Later, at the end of the season, the corn is cut, apples ripen and blackberries glisten on every bush.

Blackberry and apple camping crumble

The great thing about blackberries is that they are easily identified. Watch out for the prickles when picking – and try not to scoff all the berries before you get back to camp! Don't use blackberries that have grown on roadsides where they are exposed to traffic pollution.

> Freshly picked blackberries
> 1 or 2 cooking apples, cored and sliced
> Handful rolled oats
> Handful brown sugar
> Good knob of butter
> Nuts of your choice, roughly chopped

Melt a little butter in a saucepan, add the sliced apples and cook until tender. Add the blackberries and heat through. Meanwhile, melt a generous knob of butter in a hot pan, chuck in the oats and nuts and fry until golden, then sprinkle over some sugar to taste. Serve on top of the fruit.

Summer wildlife

- By rivers and ponds dragon- and damselflies fly.
- Look out for young birds making their first flights
- Hobbies, little birds of prey, float over green pastures.
- Tufted ducks, colourful jays, harvest mice and grass snakes are just some of the busy wildlife to look out for.
- Bees give music to the day as they hunt on heather-laden moors. Be sure to try some of their honey if you're in the right area.
- Grasshoppers and crickets hide in the long grass, playing their chirping fiddles in the midday sun.
- On dewy summer nights female glow worms climb the grass and seductively twirl their tail lamps.
- Millions of pisan snails cling to plants on coastal paths.
- Feathers are found as birds loose their coats and birdsong decreases.
- Cinnabar and magpie moths join painted ladies and red admiral butterflies to flit about the campsites.

Extra-nice things about camping in summer
- The lovely smell of summer, cut grass, hay making, meadow flowers, a cool wood, a sea breeze and the smell of the ground warming as the day unfolds.
- Sticky, sultry weather means you can cool off with a dip in sea or stream.
- Sunset in midsummer is later in the evenings and the afterglow seems to linger for longer.
- The full moon hangs low in the sky and seems huge against the horizon. The skies are clearer, so are full of twinkling stars.
- Daisy chains and dandelion clocks.
- Warm mornings with cool dew on bare feet.
- Tips of leaves and grass turn golden, giving the world a polished, sunkissed glow.
- Shooting stars.
- Staying up late.
- Wearing T-shirts from morning till night.

Autumn

Soon the leaves begin to fall and woods wear a picturesque blanket of autumn colours. If you're lucky enough to encounter a warm spell, camping on the comfortable springy layers of pine needles is a fragrant joy.

Falling leaves

Sycamore and birch turn bright yellow. Beech and oak become a deeper shade of bronze and chestnut shines golden orange. A dry summer produces the best autumnal colour.

Sycamore seeds trickle down, spinning like propeller blades in flight.

Sweet chestnuts and conkers fall.

Roasted sweet chestnuts

Not to be confused with conkers, sweet chestnuts have lots more spines on their husks. You can tell they're ripe when they are glossy and brown and take on a delicious sweetness when roasted over the campfire.

Slit all bar one of the chestnuts' skins and put them in the hot ash of the camp fire. When the un-slit chestnut explodes the others are cooked. The explosion will be reasonably fierce, so sit away from the fire and make sure there are no tents nearby. The cooked chestnuts will be very hot so be careful when peeling. Try them dipped in a bit of salt or sugar.

Mushroom hunting

Fairy rings appear in meadows – these are actually a type of fungus called the fairy ring champignon which grows in circles.

Indeed, fungi pop up everywhere.

Mushroom hunting is addictive and when you find one it's like striking gold. Do make sure you take along a really good mushroom-identification book (and learn the poisonous ones first) or better still an experienced mushroom hunter. Mushrooms prefer rich soils and short grass. Look for ponies – as the old saying goes, 'where there's muck there's mushies'.

Remember that mushrooms tend to taste as they smell; so if it smells of rotting fish or ink, reject it or you're guaranteed a tummy upset. If your mushroom smells pleasant, as a mushroom should, or of marzipan, like the horse mushroom does, you are likely to be in the clear. If in doubt just don't even go there!

The best way to eat freshly picked mushies is to simply fry them in a little butter and serve them hot on thick slices of your favourite toast.

More dew on grass means cobwebs give off an enchanting sparkle.

The rowan bears red berries and the deadly nightshade reveals its glossy black poisonous fruits.

The prickly blackthorn bush is dotted with purple-blue sloes with a powdery bloom.

Mama Carr's sloe gin

One of the nicest rituals of our last proper canvas camp of the year is picking the sloes needed to make the scrumptious sloe gin for the next year's camping trips. Don't be tempted to sample the harvest, as the raw fruits are very astringent (but don't worry – this will be totally transformed by the gin's magic touch). Pick your sloes after the first frost (usually October or November) so their skins will be softer.

> 1 bottle cheap gin (acquire 1 empty bottle about the same size)
> Freshly picked sloes
> Sugar

Prick the sloes with a fork. Empty the gin into a jug and half fill both bottles with the sloes. Add enough sugar to cover them, shaking it down as you go. Divide the gin between the two bottles and shake well. Leave the bottles where you can see them and give them a good shake every time you pass – this helps the sugar to dissolve. Drink at your first spring camp.

Traveller's joy seeds start to turn fluffy, giving it its winter name of old man's beard. Fields are ploughed. The season ends with a spectacular leaf fall coating forest floors with all the colours of autumn.

Autumn wildlife

- Amazing displays of migrating birds flocking are abundant. Some are heading south to warmer climates while others are seeking refuge from the cold Arctic winter. Among them are fieldfares, goldfinches and chaffinches.
- Bees cluster around the green blooms of the ivy.
- Kestrels hunt for their dinners. Listen out for their distinctive (kee kee kee) call.
- The last swift is seen.
- Badgers grow fat, storing up energy for the cold winter. Because there is less cover for them to hide away in, autumn is a great time of year to spot them. Stay up after dark and you may catch site of badgers foraging for blackberries and fallen apples; increase your chances further by sitting for a while, still and quiet, near to well-worn badger trails.
- The vain pied wagtail twitters away and bobs its tireless tail at its own reflection in water, windows and shiny cars.
- Squirrels squirrel away their winter stores.

Extra-nice things about camping in autumn

The earthy smell of woodland and ploughed fields.

Leaves floating down around you.

Early autumn remains warm for quite a while; extra woollies are packed just in case

but are used only for feeling cosy on gold-tinged evenings.

The campsites are empty again.

Insects almost disappear, while butterflies and bees linger.

There is lots of wild food to collect.

Peace and quiet as nature drifts off to sleep for another year.

Badger-spotting.

Winter

Bonfire night marks the start of the winter. Hats and gloves come out the cupboard; clocks go back and the days are shorter. You'll need winter provisions and plenty of courage to brave the season under canvas; if you're running low on either why not hire a pretty cottage near a deserted beach instead – just you, your lover and a crackling open fire.

Quiet beauty
- Nature sleeps, awaiting the touch of sunshine that spring brings.
- Cold spells bring hoar frosts when ice crystals form on branches, twigs and grasses producing a magical winter scene on a bright morning.
- Trees are stripped of their leaves and their inner structures revealed; moss blankets damp spaces.
- Mistletoe and holly brighten up the hedgerows.
- The hogweed's dried seed-head attracts birds.

Winter wildlife
- Flocks of birds gathering to feed from large roosts to keep warm.
- Robins and blackbirds explore gardens. The robin is said to be a good prophet of the weather: when storms are near he sings from hedges or bushes; when the weather is good he sings in the open.
- Birds of prey such as red kites and sparrowhawks drift along the air currents looking for their next meal. With no foliage for them to hide in, this is a great time to spot birds.
- Birdsong is quieter but occasionally breaks the silence on a snowy walk.
- Towards the end of the season moles are active and new molehills dot the fields.

Extra-nice things about camping in winter

- There is a cosy, safe feeling to being tucked up in your duvet.
- You can still have a bonfire which means you can sit, eat and laugh outside on calm nights.
- Good days bring blue sky and sunshine so you can wrap up warm and go for long walks.
- The stars go on forever in clear skies.

beech

sweet chestnut

silver birch

oak

walnut

field maple

elm

sycamore

ash

wild cherry

rowan

horse chestnut

BEDSTRAW HAWK MOTH
moths heat up for flight by fluttering their wings

GARDEN TIGER MOTH
there are 140,000 species of moth

TORTOISESHELL
moths spin a cocoon, butterflies emerge from a chrysalis.

APOLLO
if the first butterfly you see in the year is white you'll have good luck throughout the year

LIME HAWK MOTH
moths can be pretty too

COMMA
caterpillars have over 4000 separate muscles

LARGE WHITE
butterflies prefer pink, yellow, red or purple flowers

ORANGE TIP
the largest butterfly in the world has a 30cm wingspan

EMPEROR MOTH
moths like to headbutt light sources

BLACK VEINED WHITE
there are 24,000 species of butterfly

SIX SPOT BLUE BURNET MOTH
this moth is one of the few moths that fly in the day time

ROSY UNDERWING MOTH
moths have hairy bodies to keep them warm

SMALL COPPER
butterflies smell with their antennae

COMMON BLUE
if you find three butterflies together it's a sign of good luck.

CAMBERWELL BEAUTY
some butterflies only live for a day some live for up to eleven months.

ELEPHANT HAWK MOTH
moths fly at night

SWALLOWTAIL
the swallowtail is Britains largest butterfly - up to 8cm wide

PAINTED LADY
butterfly in welsh is "pili pala"

BRIMSTONE
butterflies taste with their feet

LARGE SKIPPER
butterflies suck nectar through a long, coiled, straw-like tongue

RED ADMIRAL
butterflies heat up for flight by sunbathing

PURPLE EMPEROR
butterflies don't have lungs

MAGPIE MOTH
butterflies used to be know as flutter-bys

PEACOCK
all butterflies have six legs and feet

field scabious (gypsy rose)

pyramidal orchid

ladys bedstraw

rye grass

ox-eye daisy

spear thistle

field poppy

Love the world we're in

'Help protect the countryside by being aware that, while you are there, you are a visitor. When you visit a friend, you take care to leave your friends home just as you found it. You would never think of trampling garden flowers, chopping down trees in the yard, putting soap in the drinking water, or writing your name on the living-room wall. When you visit the country, the same courtesies apply. Please take all your rubbish home and leave everything just as you found it.'

Scout lore

Country lore

Shut farm gates if you find them shut and leave open if you find them open.

Always climb over a gate at the hinge end; better still find a stile.

Keep your dog on a lead if you are anywhere near sheep and cattle.

Don't pull wildflowers up by the roots.

Don't light any fires unless you have permission to do so.

Always take your rubbish away with you; never drop litter.

Never trample across crops.

Walk on the same side of the road as oncoming traffic.

Dandelion folklore

Dandelion clocks have the most amazing talents and are working hard throughout the summer not only to tell you the time, but also to warn you of bad weather and make all your dreams come true.

'He loves me, he loves me not'

Folklore says that blowing a dandelion clock will tell you if you're loved or not. Apparently if you can blow all the seeds off in one go you are loved passionately. If some seeds remain your lover has a few doubts; if lots remain you are not loved at all.

Blowing clocks

Some say that the number of blows it takes to free all the seeds of a dandelion clock directly correlates to the hour of the day. Exhaustive tests by the happy campers have shown that this method of time-telling isn't always 100 per cent accurate.

Wish upon a dandelion

If you catch a fairy (a dandelion seed), make a wish and send it back on its journey again to make your wish come true. It is also said that blowing the seeds off a dandelion clock will carry your thoughts and dreams to your loved one. Get blowing . . .

Dandelion weathermen

Dandelion clocks are said to be excellent weathermen. When the dandelions have gone to seed keep a close eye on them. In fine weather the ball extends to its fullest, but when the rain approaches it shuts like an umbrella.

Weather – happy signs

Easterly winds generally bring dry weather – hot in summer, cold in winter.

Both early-morning mists and dew in summer are omens for a fine sunny day and will dry up as the sun climbs higher in the sky.

Crickets tend to chirp more when the sun is shining, so listen out. They also make great thermometers: count the number of chirps a cricket makes in fifteen seconds, then add thirty-seven; the sum will be very close to the outside temperature in fahrenheit.

'When dew is on the grass, rain will never come to pass;
When grass is dry at morning light, look for rain before the night'
Fair weather with clear skies and calm winds usually means that the temperature will cool at night, resulting in the formation of dew early in the morning. Rainy weather is associated with rising air, which means no dew is produced.

Haze usually indicates fine weather; the longer the fine spell lasts the thicker the haze. Sometimes haze forms a cloud and pretends to be an approaching storm.

'Swallows high, staying dry; swallows low, wet will blow'
During fine weather, insects are carried up high on warm thermal currents so birds fly high for their dinner. Also, high air pressure makes it easier for birds to fly at a higher altitude.
    If the beach is covered in a cold, clammy blanket of fog, try coming inland a few miles and you will often find the sky is perfectly clear.

If there is a sea breeze and a clear sky you're probably best off sticking to the beach because the clouds have been blown inland.

Sea mist moving inland in the evening on a light wind means nice weather the following day.

'Rain before seven, fine before eleven'
Rain that falls during the night is usually frontal rain. Frontal rain normally lasts for no more than three or four hours in any one place; on that basis, rain before seven should indeed pass by eleven.

'Red sky at night, shepherds' delight; red sky in the morning, shepherds' warning'
Clouds shine red in the evening when sunlight from the west lights up rain clouds moving away to the east. If the morning skies are red, it is likely that clear skies to the east let the sun light up the bellies of rain clouds coming in from the west.

Cirrostratus
Very high, white, wispy veil, almost transparent and forms a halo around the sun.
If you're lucky you might see the sky smiling – nerds call it a 'circumzenithal arc'
but we just point and say, 'look, everyone, an upside-down rainbow.'

CLOUD MAP

cirrus

cirrostratus

high

cumulo nimbus

altocumulus

altostratus

mid

stratocumulus

cumulus

nimbostratus

stratus

low

Weather – unhappy signs

If the sky has a ragged look about it, it is usually because of a pesky strong wind; in summer this generally means imminent bad weather.

Westerly winds usually bring moisture-laden air, meaning rain.
Southwesterly winds blowing unevenly or strongly are particularly notorious.
Northeasterly winds bring sunny conditions to the west coast but cool conditions to the east coast.

'Mares' tails and mackerel scales make tall ships carry low sails'
Feathery cirrus or mare's tails high in the sky are the first sign that a weather front is on the way. If they trail downwards, the clouds are rising and the weather will be fine. But if the tails bend upwards and appear aside the unmistakable mackerel skies it means the clouds are moving downward and rain is coming.

It's a sure sign of rain ahead when the air is unusually clear and distant objects stand out starkly and brightly coloured with a sort of floodlit glow about them. This is one of the most reliable indications that there is and is quite unmistakable when you have learnt to recognise it.

'Cows lying down is a sure sign of rain'
This old favourite is untrue. Sometimes cows just like to lie down, chat about life and generally chew the cud. However . . .

'A cow with its tail to the west makes the weather best,
A cow with its tail to the east makes the weather least'
Cows, being sensible folk, prefer not to have the wind blowing in their faces, and so typically stand with their backs to the wind. Since westerly winds by and large mean arriving or continuing fair weather and easterly winds usually suggest arriving or continuing unsettled weather, a cowvane is as good a way as any of knowing what the weather will be up to for the next little while.

'The reddish moon has water in her eye; before too long you won't be dry'
The red colour is caused by dust being pushed ahead of a low-pressure front bringing wet weather.

A pine cone is a good indicator of weather to have in your campsite because it closes up in moist weather to protect its seeds.

Clouds

Cirrus
Very high, delicate, white and wispy. Sometimes described as mares' tails because it looks a bit like locks of hair floating serenely along. Cirrus generally indicates fair to pleasant weather, but its growing thicker and scruffier signals the approach of a warm front carrying moisture-laden air so watch out for rain in a day or so.

Cirrocumulus
Very high, white, separated, small and heaped. This is the cloud in a mackerel sky. Most of the time it just hangs out on sunny days, making pretty patterns with cirrus and cirrostratus.

Altostratus
High, white and layered. The sky looks milky and the sun can only just be seen. When very thick it may lead to light rain or snow, but sometimes at sunrise and sunset it reflects the sun and glows with all its heart.

Nimbostratus
Low and dark, a blanket that has been thrown over the sun bringing seemingly never-ending heavy rain.

Stratus
Low, white layer cloud that brings no rain but annoys us when she shades the sun in the form of fog and mists – spoilsport.

Altocumulus
Masses of small, loose balls of bright white cotton-wool high up in the sky. Is sometimes confused with cirrocumulus or a mackerel sky, but these little fellas have larger gaps in between them. Its appearance on a humid summer morning often points to late-afternoon thunderstorms.

Cumulonimbus
Dark and looming. Hovers near to the ground and stretches up high into the sky with an anvil-shaped top. Almost certain to bring rain and if you're very unlucky thunder and lightning too, so retreat to the pub when you see it coming.

Cumulus
Low, white, fluffy cartoon cloud that appears in fair weather, perfect for kicking back and making cloud shapes.

Stratocumulus
Low, dull and lumpy, forming in rolls or waves covering the sky. It looks threatening but only means rain if it's very thick; in fact quite often it means that fine weather is on the way.

Oh, we do like to be beside the seaside

Beachcombing

As children we were devoted to running along the shoreline, excitedly pointing out nature's treasures, marvelling at the size of a beached jellyfish and gathering up seashells to listen into. Even now, as grown-ups (allegedly), whenever we're on a beach curiosity sends us head-down with the roar of the sea in our ears. It's like a form of meditation.

Go find yourself some treasure. Any rubbish that floats is likely to end up on the strandline along with long hollow fronds of mermaid's tresses and crab shells discarded whole, empty or with legs intact when they've become too tight a fit. On rocky beaches the egg cases of the whelk, papery 'sea wash' balls, bounce along in the wind. If you're lucky you'll spot mermaids' purses, the egg-case of skates and rays, which are said to bring good fortune. While you're there create yourself some good karma and take some rubbish home with you.

Rock pooling

Recently we rediscovered rock pooling and spent an excited day seeing who could catch the biggest, most impressive creature with our seaside nets and buckets. We were amazed at the amount of life in these tiny ecosystems. Along with shoals of miniature fish we spotted sea squirts and anemones and even tracked down a starfish holed up under a rock. A particularly grumpy rock fish was taken into custody along with a fidgety crab and a tiny fish that suckered itself to the side of the bucket like some sort of prehistoric creature whose legs hadn't yet fully evolved.

After our expedition we gently returned our finds to the rock pools and wished them luck in the rapidly incoming tide. There's arguably nothing better than being a kid again.

Crabbing

The best time to go crabbing is at high tide on a jetty or alongside a harbour wall. Take a long piece of string or fishing line and tie a small stone to the end. A little further up attach a piece of bait (crabs find fish, chicken or bacon rind delicious). Lower the line into the water and when you feel a little tug, slowly and carefully pull up the string and scoop the crabs into a waiting net or bucket.

Have a crab race: draw a circle in the sand and race them from the centre. Betting is essential. Go for the rank outsider; he may have one less leg but he must be feisty – he's survived without it after all. Don't forget to return your crabs to where you found them at the end of the day.

Life on the waves

On Lunga Island off the west coast of Scotland the puffins are so tame they will even come up to say hello. On the east coast of Scotland lies the Isle of May, which is home to thousands of puffins, kittiwakes and razorbills. Further south take a trip to Lundy Island off the coast of North Devon; the puffins aren't as widespread as they used to be but there is a nice pub in which to replenish after your expedition.

The Farne Islands off the coast of Northumberland are the breeding ground of tens of thousands of puffins and thousands of kittiwake, Arctic tern and guillemot. In the waters surrounding them are an estimated 2,000 Atlantic grey seals, with their big Roman noses. You can also spot their distinctive faces off the coast of Ceredigion in Wales.

Late spring and summer are the best viewing times for dolphins. Cardigan Bay on the west coast of Wales has a resident population of bottlenose dolphins and the Isle of Mull off the west coast of Scotland has dolphins, minke whales and basking sharks.

Make some memories . . .

Beauty products from nature

Raid your camp kitchen to make yourself and your mates look even more beautiful. Always test on a small area first to rule out allergic reaction.

Face packs
Strawberry mask (oily skin)
Mash three large strawberries within an inch of their lives. Apply to the face and neck and leave for ten minutes. Rinse off to find the skin sparkling.

Banana mask (dry to normal skin)
Mash up a very ripe banana, add a little honey and a couple of spoons of oatmeal if you have it. Apply to face and hair and leave for about five minutes, then gently wash off and feel your skin tingle.

Avocado mask
Mash up the flesh of one avocado and apply to your face. Leave for fifteen to twenty minutes (try not to eat it off). Wash your face with cold water to close the pores. A very nourishing treat for parched skin.

Skin shiners
Mix two tablespoons of honey with two teaspoons of milk. Smooth over face and neck and leave on for ten minutes. Rinse off with warm water.

Mix together a tablespoon of oats, a tablespoon of honey and a tablespoon of yoghurt. Rub into your skin to gently exfoliate, then leave on for a couple of minutes. Rinse off with warm water.

A natural wrinkle remover
Simply cut a few grapes in half and gently rub the flesh into your face and neck. Wait about fifteen or twenty minutes before rinsing off.

Hair shiner
Stir a teaspoon of honey into four cups of warm water, add a squeeze of lemon if you're blonde or some crushed rosemary if you're brunette. After shampooing, pour mixture through hair; don't rinse out – just dry as usual.

Foot reviver
After a hard day's walking, treat yourself to a foot spa. Put some hot (not too hot) water in a bucket or bowl, then add some sea salt, some lavender oil and some crushed rosemary. Place your feet inside and relax.

Nature's remedies

Herb teas

Herb teas are a really gentle way to ease many symptoms. You can use herb teabags but better still if you can find the herb growing wild in its natural state just rinse well, steep in hot water for about five minutes and allow to cool before drinking slowly. Add a little honey to sweeten if you wish.

Chamomile tea is great for stress and anxiety. Its calming properties make it the perfect bedtime drink, helping you to get a restful night's sleep. You can also use cold chamomile tea on minor burns and scalds and cooled teabags on the eyes to freshen and reduce puffiness.

Dandelion tea is a great tonic for hangovers, so always useful after a few too many around the campfire.

Fresh thyme tea is a great remedy for freshening breath. Make a mouthwash by steeping some in hot water and letting it cool. Chewing on mint or parsley leaves will do the same thing.

Rosemary tea helps to relieve digestive complaints and is very uplifting.

Sage tea helps calm sore throats, sore tonsils and bleeding gums.

We've all experienced nettle stings, so seek revenge by making a cup of nettle tea. This iron-enriched tonic cleanses the blood, helps ease arthritis, soothes eczema and tastes surprisingly good. Soak some young nettle tops in cold water for a few minutes while you put the kettle on, then put in a teapot or cup and pour over hot water, leaving to infuse for five minutes before drinking.

Other good stuff

Dock leaves soothe nettle stings. Where you find nettles you will usually find dock leaves growing alongside – they're like the good cop/bad cop of the plant world. Just rub on to the affected area.

Lemon is fantastic; it's a very powerful natural antiseptic and can be used in many ways:

- Drink warm water with a slice of lemon first thing in the morning to cleanse your system and flush out your kidneys.
- For a cold at camp a glass of hot water with honey and lemon juice is a traditional remedy. Add some chopped or grated fresh ginger for extra clout.
- To ease nausea, drink the juice of half a lemon in a pint of hot water.
- If you have earache squeeze a couple of drops of lemon juice on to a piece of warmed cotton-wool and plug the ear with it.
- Dab a bit of lemon on your pimples before bed to dry them up.

Garlic is a natural antifungal, antibacterial and anti-inflammatory. It's a great remedy for colds, coughs and flu. Eat it raw in food. Our friend Jane swears by eating a clove of garlic in an apple when she has a cold; if you can't face that try our hummus recipe on page 125. Also try rubbing a clove on your spots to reduce the infection.

Camping first-aid kit

- Arnica cream for bruises
- Distilled witch-hazel for sunburn, minor burns, bruises, insect bites and spots
- Bach's rescue remedy, great for shock and sunstroke
- Lavender oil for minor burns, scalds and spots; also relieves headaches and repels insects

food for the soul

Camping yoga

Salutations to the sun (surya namaskara)

We all need a good stretch after a night under canvas and yoga is a great way to start the day. The sun salutation is series of postures that gently works all of your muscles and organs, this particular version is based on hatha yoga. You can do it at any time but first thing in the morning is best, before you fill up on breakfast. Find yourself a flat bit of ground, face the sun and lay down your mat or blanket. Don't worry if you all you end up in a heap laughing – it's all part of the fun and just as beneficial; laughter, as they say, is the elixir of life.

1. Prayer pose
Standing, close your eyes and put your palms together.
Put your feet together and relax.
Breathe and feel the sun's warmth.

2. Raised arms – inhale
Raise and stretch both your arms above your head.
Keep your arms separated, shoulder-width apart.
Bend your head, arms and upper body backwards; push your hips forwards.

3. Hand to feet – exhale
Bend forward from the hips until the fingers or palms of your hands touch the floor on either side of your feet.
Aim (not essential) to touch your knees with your forehead.
Don't strain; do try to keep your knees straight.

4. Horse – inhale
Stretch your right leg back and place the palms of your hands flat on the floor beside your feet.
Stretch your right leg back as far as possible and put your knee on the ground.
At the same time, bend your left knee keeping the left foot on the floor in the same position.
Keep your arms straight, and your head and back arched backwards.

5. Downward dog – exhale
Take your left leg back and put your left foot back beside your right foot.
Simultaneously raise your bum and lower your head between your arms; relax your neck so the back and legs form two sides of a triangle.
Try to lower your heels towards the floor, bring your shoulders blades down your back and push your hands into the ground.

6. Salute with eight points – hold your breath
Lower your knees, chest and chin to the floor.
Only your knees, chest, hands and chin touch the floor.
Keep your bum, hips and abdomen raised.

7. Cobra – inhale
Raise your torso and arch your back.
Lower your bum and hips towards the floor.
Push your chest forwards and bend your head back.
Keep your elbows bent and tight into your body, relax your shoulders.
Your thighs and hips remain on the floor and your arms support your upper body.

8. Downward dog – exhale
Raise your bum to the sky and repeat pose 5.

9. Horse – inhale while going into the pose
Same as pose 4.

10. Hand to feet – exhale
Same as pose 3.

11. Raised arms – inhale while straightening your body
Same as pose 2.

12. Prayer – exhale while assuming the final position.
Same as pose 1.

This is half of one round. In the second half you repeat the poses but start with your left leg. This makes one complete sun salutation. Aim to keep the poses flowing into each other and complete ten rounds in all. It may seem like a lot but will get you really warmed up – more importantly, you will feel so virtuous and pure that you will feel fine about having two breakfasts.

Make some art

Recipe for preserving children*

1 grass-grown field
Half a dozen children (or more)
Several dogs (and puppies if available)
1 brook
Pebbles

Method
Into the field pour the children and dogs, allowing to mix well.
Pour brook over pebbles till slightly frothy.
When children are nicely brown, leave to cool in the water.
When dry, serve with milk and fresh campfire biscuits (see page 169).

*Found on the inside of a yellow tin for index cards, labelled recipes.

Make cloud shapes

tents up, I should really go and help them but I'm trying to
look busy by telling everyone I'm writing stuff for the boo
OK I'm off they're all throwing water all over me!
Aug 17th Yesterday was one of the best days ever... a hard da
of having all day fun, volleyball, beach Olympics (Kam won - wh
a surprise!) human pyramids, well more like a human pile! All th
ladies made a fantastic beach feast we grilled the fresh macke
that we had hunted and gathered at the local fishmonger
It was delicious mmmmm!
We hardly noticed how late it had got until we looked lo
and realised that the beach had emptied, Only a few surfers
left bobbing about in the sea looking like seals. The sun h
started to go down, the wine had begun to take effect and w
were all starting to pack up when someone shouted "last one
in the sea has to make breakfast!" Without hesitation we loo
at each other, looked at the sea, stripped off and raced in starker
it was hilarious, no thoughts of wobbly bits now, the most
important thing was preserving our lie in! We all had the b
gest beaming faces I have ever seen, we must have looked like
bunch of raving loonys. The boys holding onto their bits and the g
holding onto their boobs I noticed that Soph was running next
me struggling to control hers, Kats were behaving perfectly
while I'd given up with mine. We reached the shoreline and div
in head first. It felt amazing as we splashed about swimming
free, still smiling ... I love skinny dipping!
Apart from the walk back - we spotted a group of bird spotters
on the top of the cliff in their matching regulation anoraks a
binoculars - pointing them straight at us! Instead of calmly
walking back (they'd seen us now anyhow!) we made a mad
and literally jumped on our clothes desperately trying to get m
legs into dry trousers. It was no use we just collapsed into hils
laughter! Looking forward to my brekkie - Thanks Grace!

A trip to visit the sunset

It's a magical walk and it makes the sunset all the more special. Whether there are just two of you hand in hand or a group of happy friends browned from the day's sun it's a beautiful way to end many a perfect day.

Grab a blanket, a bottle of river-chilled champagne, some glasses and a good bar of chocolate. Take a walk to a good viewing spot – a hilltop, mountain ridge, beach or maybe even a tree branch. Once you've caught your breath settle down and appreciate the ever-changing kaleidoscope sky until every drop of colour has been squeezed out and replaced with zillions of twinkling stars.

A tale of campfire magic

We'd eaten our feast, we'd played silly games, sung songs and shared a few secrets. As the sun made its way sleepily to bed and stars filled the sky just the murmur of campers deep in conversation could be heard. It was the perfect point in the evening to hand round the wishing powder. If a wish was to come true they would see a sign and if not they would see only the glow of the embers. Everyone took a small handful of the powder, made a wish to themselves and threw the powder on to the flickering flames. Time after time a scattering of bright twinkling sparks flew out of the fire bringing wide smiles to all. Being good folk their wishes did come true. In fact our small friend Ollie tells us that the Lego appeared the very next day.

To make your campfire twinkle like the stars, throw on a handful of ordinary granulated sugar. You can also sprinkle on iron filings, if you can get your hands on any, to give you a scattering of twinkling gold sparks. A handful of salt will make the flames glow a dazzling orange and potassium chloride (you can often find it in salt substitutes) will turn the flames a glittering purple. Always make sure that you stand back from the fire after you have thrown on the wishing powder.

Shooting stars

'Like a bolt out of the blue, fate steps in and sees you thru;
When you wish upon a star, your dreams come true'

Some native American tribes called shooting stars 'children of the moon', in the belief that they were fragments of lunar material. In Chinese culture shooting stars were thought to be dragons or messengers sent from the heavens; and they were explained in Siberian legends with the notion that the gods would peer through a dome of sewn hides exposing flashes of the heavens hidden beyond.

In fact, when comets fly through space they leave behind a trail of dust and ice. If the earth crosses this trail as it spins around the sun these fragments, usually no larger than a tiny grain of sand, burn up in our atmosphere and create meteors or shooting stars.

Seeing a shooting star is a truly wonderful experience and it's a tradition for us to watch out for them with a bottle of bubbly – it seems fitting, given that Dom Perignon is quoted as saying at the moment he discovered champagne, 'come quickly, I am tasting stars!'

You can see shooting stars on most nights but at certain times of the year spectacular meteor showers happen and shooting stars can be seen literally raining out of the sky.

Improve your chances of seeing a shower of stars
- Meteor showers are named after the constellation from which they appear, so have a look at the star map to help you work out where you should be looking.
- Relax your eyes and don't look in any specific spot.
- Get yourself away from any man-made light.
- The moonlight will swallow up all but the brightest shooting stars so the best time to go star hunting is on a night of a new moon. If the new moon coincides with a major meteor shower you're in for a treat.
- As the earth rotates, the side facing the direction of the orbit around the sun runs into more dust, this direction is directly overhead at dawn so you will see twice as many shooting stars in the few hours before dawn as you will just after sunset. So for a really magical experience set your alarm and take a very early candlelit walk.
- Perseid, a star shower that gives one of the best displays, takes place in august which is by chance the perfect time of year for camping. As you will already be situated in the best possible place for stargazing, the great big outdoors, it's the perfect opportunity to catch a falling star.

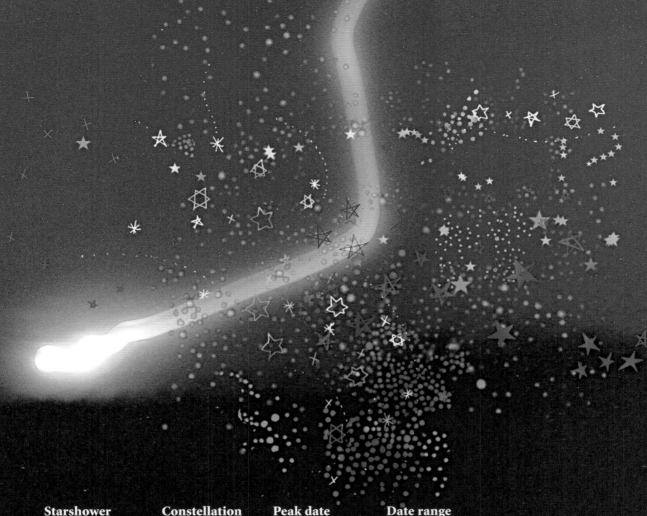

Starshower	Constellation	Peak date	Date range
Quadrantids	Ursa Major	3 January	1 to 6 January
Lyrids	Lyra	22 April	19 to 25 April
Spring Aquarids	Aquarius	6 May	1 to 10 May
Summer Aquarids	Aquarius	29 July	26 to 31 July
Perseids	Perseus	12 August	23 July to 25 August
Orionids	Orion	22 October	16 to 22 October
Taurids	Taurus	5 November	20 October to 30 November
Leonids	Leo	17 November	15 to 20 November
Geminids	Gemini	13 December	7 to 15 December

STAR MAP

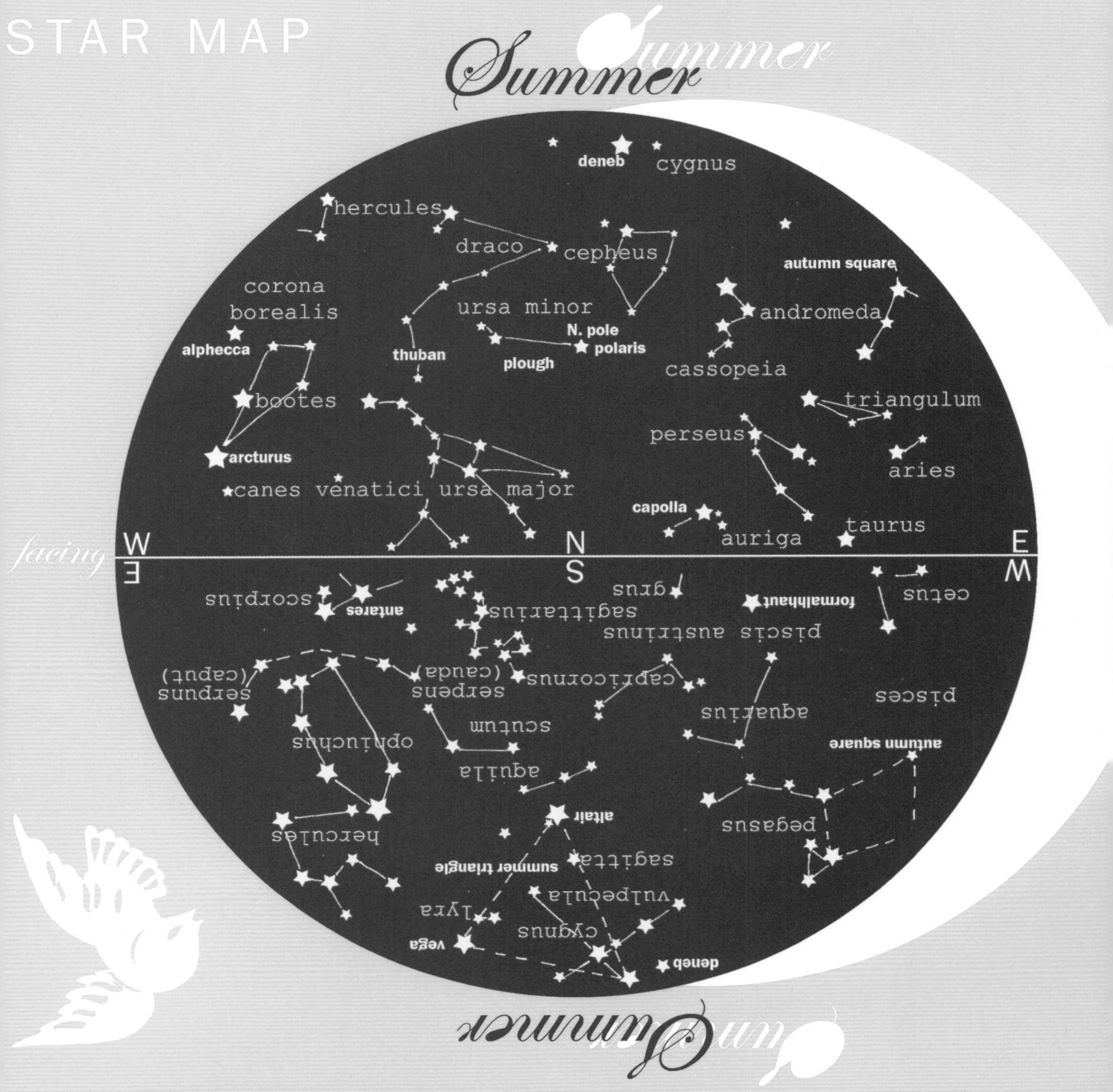

Summer
deneb
cygnus
hercules
draco
cepheus
autumn square
corona borealis
ursa minor
andromeda
N. pole
polaris
alphecca
thuban
plough
cassopeia
bootes
triangulum
perseus
arcturus
aries
canes venatici
ursa major
capolla
taurus
auriga
facing
W
N
E
E
S
W
scorpius
antares
sagittarius
grus
formalhaut
cetus
piscis austrinus
serpens (caput)
serpens (cauda)
capricornus
pisces
aquarius
scutum
ophiuchus
autumn square
aquila
altair
pegasus
hercules
summer triangle
sagitta
vulpecula
lyra
cygnus
vega
deneb
Summer

Starry-eyed? How to read the star map:

In order to have the best views of the sky, you should try to find somewhere with as little light around as possible to minimise light pollution (any light around you which prevents your eyes from adjusting to the dark, therefore making star-gazing more difficult). If you can, get a red flashlight, or place some red cellophane or sweet wrapper over the lens of a standard flashlight. When you shine it on the map, your night vision won't be as affected as with a white light.

Work out which way is north by searching for the North star, also known as Polaris. The easiest way to do this is to look for the constellation Ursa Minor, sometimes known as the Little Dipper or Little Bear (it looks a bit like a saucepan with a handle). Follow the two stars at the end of the basin upward. This should lead you directly to Polaris. Because the Earth is constantly moving, the position of the stars alters – so make sure you're looking at the right map for the time of year. Orient the sky map with the N pointed towards north. Now locate Polaris on the map and you're ready to set off on your exploration. By turning the map upside-down and facing in the opposite direction (south) you can explore the entire night sky. Good luck star hunting x

Winter

capola
perseus
lynx
triangulum
ursa major
leo
andromeda
cassiopeia
polaris
N. pole
ursa minor
plough
cepheus
draco
canes venatici
autumn square
pegasus
spring trapezium
deneb
cygnus
bootes

W — N — S — E   facing

columba
spica
hydra
lepus
cetus   eridanus   canis major
pisces
sirius
rigel
winter hexagon
spring trapezium
orion
regulus
aries
procyon
taurus
aldebaran
cancer
leo
canis minor
perseus
pollux
auriga   gemini
castor
capella

Some popular constellations and when they're visible:

- Andromeda: the chained princess, visible all year.
- Canis Major: the greater dog, contains Sirium, the brightest star in the entire sky; visible December to April.
- Cassiopeia: the queen; beautiful and devoted wife of King Cepheus and mother of Andromeda; visible all year.
- Monoceros: the unicorn; has magical powers; visible December to April.
- Orion: the hunter; boasted he could kill any animal on earth but was fatally stung by a scorpion; visible November to April.
- Pegasus: the winged horse; mythical creature born from the love of Neptune's tears; visible July to February.
- Perseus: the hero; heroically rescued (and later married) Andromeda from the clutches of the sea monster; visible all year.
- Cetus: visible all year.
- Ursa Major: the Great Bear, also known as the Plough, or the Big Dipper; visible all year.

Sleeping on a beach . . .

. . . An amazing thing to do if you're on a romantic weekend away. It's so magical to sleep under the stars and hear the ocean lapping in your dreams.

This is only recommended in summer as it's too chilly in winter. Remember to check the weather for a clear night and choose your beach carefully; the more secluded the better, and sandy beaches are comfier. Be sure to make your bed above the shoreline. Find a spot and smooth the sand. Put down a blanket, then a sheet and finally your duvet and pillows. The bed will get damp on the outside when the dew drops so make your bed at sundown, when the sand is still hot, and it will be toasty and dry on the inside. Enjoy the peace and wonder, go to bed early and indulge in your good fortune. Zzzz . . .

How, what, where

www.thehappycampers.co.uk

Getting there
www.multimap.com
www.theaauk.co.uk
www.rac.co.uk/routeplanner

General camping
www.campingandcaravanningclub.co.uk
www.campingmagazine.co.uk
www.worldofcamping.co.uk

British campsite listings and reviews
www.ukcampsite.co.uk
www.caravancampingsites.co.uk
www.campinguk.com
www.caravancampingsites.co.uk

Wild Camping
www.mountaineering-
scotland.org.uk/leaflets/wildcamp.html
www.dartmoor-npa.gov.uk/camping_booklet.pdf
www.go4awalk.com/ask/wildcamping
www.wild-adventures.co.uk/camping.htm
www.campinginthelakes.co.uk/wildcamping

Weather
www.bbc.co.uk/weather
www.metoffice.com
www.cloudappreciationsociety.org

European campsites
www.interhike.com
www.campingfrance.com
www.camping.it (Italy)
www.campingeurope.com

Go greener
www.carbonneutral.com
www.soilassociation.org
www.howtogogreen.com
www.energysavingtrust.com

Somewhere a bit different
www.belletentscamping.co.uk

www.coldblow-camping.co.uk
www.cornishlight.co.uk/camping.htm
www.yha.org.uk
www.thebigdomain.com
www.tipis.co.uk
www.cornish-tipi-holidays.co.uk
www.relaxinwales.com
www.larkhilltipis.co.uk
www.tipi-holidays.co.uk
www.yurt-holidays.co.uk
www.devonyurtholidays.co.uk
www.northumbrianwigwams.com
www.farhousetipis.co.uk
www.tipiwest.co.uk
www.southpenquite.co.uk
www.brutonyurts.com
www.hearthworks.co.uk
www.ecoretreats.co.uk
www.yurtshop.com
www.shepherd-hut.co.uk
www.horsedrawncaravans.com
www.new-forest-gypsy-caravans.co.uk
www.underthethatch.co.uk
www.cottage-holiday-
wales.co.uk/Romanycaravanholidays
www.kamperhire.co.uk
www.campers2go.co.uk
www.coolcampervans.com
www.campervanhireuk.com
www.cornwallcampers.co.uk
www.veedubclassics.com
www.vwcamperco.com
www.rideworldwide.co.uk
www.podcaravans.com
www.canaljunction.com
www.waterscape.com
www.camp-sites.co.uk/blakes-boating-
holidays.htm
www.viking-afloat.com/barge

Festivals
www.bigchill.net
www.bestival.net
www.glastonburyfestivals.co.uk
www.big-green-gathering.com
www.efestivals.co.uk

www.virtualfestivals.com
www.tangerinefields.co.uk

Try something new
www.britsurf.co.uk
www.kitesurfing.org
www.mbuk.com
www.britishcycling.org.uk
www.worldfootbag.com
www.walkingworld.com
www.walkingbritain.co.uk
www.ramblers.org.uk
www.bcu.org.uk (canoeing)
www.canoekayak.co.uk
www.woodcraftschool.co.uk
www.tastymushroompartnership.co.uk/
    collecting
www.wildernesswood.co.uk
www.bhs.org.uk (horse riding)

Water stuff
www.river-swimming.co.uk
www.goodbeachguide.co.uk
www.sas.org.uk (surfers against sewage)
www.lidos.org.uk

Wild world
www.garden-birds.co.uk (bird sounds)
www.nationaltrust.org
www.visitbritain.com
www.enjoyengland.com
www.visitwales.com
www.visitscotland.com
www.discovernorthernireland.com
www.simplyscilly.co.uk
www.visitnorfolk.co.uk
www.thenewforest.co.uk
www.cumbria-the-lake-district.co.uk
www.beautiful-devon.co.uk
www.wildlifetrusts.org
www.british-trees.com
www.birdsofbritain.co.uk
www.britishbutterflies.co.uk
www.wildflowers.co.uk
www.glaucus.org.uk/strandlin.htm
    (beach combing)

LOMO cameras
www.lomography.com
Kat's Lomo home:
    www.lomohomes.com/littlekat
Tess's Lomo home:
    www.lomohomes.com/bigtess
Lomo repairs:
    Roger Lean Russian Camera Repairs
Telephone 020 8881 5208
Lomo facts: www.kataan.org/lomofaq

Cool stuff
Tipi tents: www.moskoselkatan.se
More tipi tents: www.albioncanvas.co.uk
www.armytents.co.uk (good tents)
More good tents www.tents-direct.co.uk
www.woodlandyurts.co.uk
www.magmabooks.com (good books)
www.gransfors.com (good axes)
www.shoefolk.com
www.folkclothing.com
www.howies.co.uk
www.leatherman.com
www.labourandwait.co.uk
www.ebay.co.uk
www.freecycle.org
www.carbootcalendar.com
www.carbootjunction.com
www.castoff.info
www.cornwall-online.co.uk/history/pasty
www.maglite.com
www.organicsheepskins.co.uk
www.everymantheatre.org.uk (Giffords circus)
www.goodnessdirect.co.uk
www.helios.co.uk
www.farmersmarkets.net
www.bigbarn.co.uk
www.bogstandard.org
www.millimetre.uk.net
www.katheyes.com
www.janephotos.com
www.myspace.com/samhare
www.strumpets.co.uk

thank you!

A massive thank you to all of our incredible friends and family who have inspired and helped us and without whom this book would not have been possible. WE LOVE YOU! Thanks for camping, laughing and putting up with our hair-brained ideas! And an especially big thanks to all of you who gave us your recipes, ideas and photos that we couldn't quite fit in this time . . . maybe in the next book!

Thanks so much to Howard and Sarah for your love, photos and giggles; to Susy and Jacko, thanks for your support and giggling a lot too – we love you all, and can you all stop living so far away please! To Dad Carr and Diana, thanks for putting us up and for the never-ending entertainment! And thanks to Dave for always being there at the right moment.

. . . and to our friends (in no particular order): to Grace, thanks for being you and the perfect camping princess; Sils, thanks for being you too and making us all laugh; to Dylan for being a brilliant bows and arrows expert and an all round lovely; to Isla for your love and for keeping us calm in times of panic; to Tara for being incredibly helpful and fun to have around; to the fantastic Mr and Mrs P. and Lumpy Bumpy for your never-ending love and support; to Georgie for all your beautiful songs; to Kat and Tom for your endless enthusiasm and love – we miss you guys! To Sam and Janey, thanks for always being there when we needed a question answered or a bed borrowed, and extra thanks to Janey for your talent – we couldn't have done it without you lady! To Ferg and Rose, lil' Ad, Soph and Patrick, for inspired summers, and also thanks for the birdies – one day we'll use them. To the Exeter crew: Andy and Lucy, James and Marie, Jon in a dress – thanks for all the great camp-outs. To Karin, Robin, Willow and North for your belief; to Jon and Liz for your great advice and to the lovely Reecy for your love and encouragement – we need to see you more! To Lisa for just being a star; to Matt for your computer skills as well as your friendship; Steph, for your potatoes as well as your friendship; to Hannah, Elen, Amber, Jojo, Gazza and Eddie for all your smiles; to Rob for all your mad book ideas and for keeping Fred sane. Big thanks to Emma Taylor (we will give the books back honest!); to Sue, thanks for lending us your house, your horses and your books; to Juliette, thanks for the mousse; to Rowan Boy and Rowan Girl; to Kam (thanks for being a life-saver!); to Polly and Shaun for helping out and being so amazing; to Matt, Sol and Ollie for all your support and for being so amazing too; to Yeelin, Matt and Madeleine, thanks for your great advice and love; to Katrina, thanks so much for your encouragement; to Mel and Katie for all your useful book advice; to Pietro for helping out; to Terry and Roger for being just wonderful, and a massive thanks to all the other Happy Campers who have starred in the book, you know who you are!

Thanks to everybody at Bloomsbury: Mike, you're a legend; Rosemary, thanks for believing in us; and Louise, Monica, Richard and Antigone, thanks for all your hard work.

Thanks to Simon and Sophie at PFD for your endless enthusiasm and encouragement and for keeping us calm in times of need.

Thanks to Leo for the poem.

Thanks to all our happy campers for their additional photos: page 12 (top photo) by Eric Heyes; page 12 (bottom photo) by Collin Carr; page 22 by Jenny Anderson; page 27 (bottom photo) by Mike Jones; page 28 by Sarah Molteno; page 38 by Lizzie Heyes; page 48 (top photo) by Solange Leon; page 48 (bottom photo) by Collin Carr; page 52 by Mike Jones; page 55 by Susila Bailey Bond; page 140 by Kat Haynes (big Kat); page 170 by Lizzie Heyes; page 178 by Karn Sandilands; page 184 by Dylan Byrne; page 192 by Lizzie Heyes; page 200 by Lizzie Heyes; page 224 by Solange Leon; page 246 by Susila Bailey-Bond.

From Tess

To my beautiful and amazing Karn, thanks for being my inspiration, for putting up with me and always being there, for your amazing carrying and helping skills and for being my hero and the love of my life . . . I love you x

To Mum, what can I say? You're the best, an inspiration – thanks a million for your love, never-ending support, amazing food and belief in me – I finally did it! Love you too x

And Fred, thanks for putting up with coming home to us working every night and having no one to play with, for looking after us and for being a superstar of a brother. Love you x

And to my little Kat, thanks darling for everything, you're amazing. I feel very proud to have you as my sister – thanks for all your genius ideas, for keeping me in line and for making this one of the most fun things I've ever done.

From Kat

To my favourite Fred, thank you for always being there for me, for putting up with all the book talk, for looking after me through the bad times and laughing with me through the good times, and most importantly for being the greatest love of my life . . . I love you x

Thanks to my beautiful sister Lizzie for always being an ear to listen. You have been a star throughout and I appreciate how much you have gone above and beyond the call of sister duties! Love you pretty lady. And to big bro Ad for volleyball, piñatas and lots of discussions.

Thanks Dad, for always looking after me and for handing down 'the tent'; to Pauline for always listening; to Grandma for your love, spelling and crossword skills; to Jen for welcoming me into your beautiful family and for always being ready to whip up a jar of something delicious for us; and to Karn, thanks for your patience and help no matter what the request.

And thanks to my partner in crime, Tess, without whom I'd have gone mad ages ago. You bring a sparkle to every day – here's to more hair-brained ideas!

. . . to Mum, thanks for being an everlasting inspiration x